日本料理

JAPANESE CUISINE

作者：陳綉麗
烹飪協助：蔡壽蓮
翻譯：史嘉琳
文稿協助：邱澄子·陳素真·張麗雯

照相：林坤鴻
設計：張方馨
打字：東奇照相打字有限公司
　　　源豐英文電腦排版社
製版：四海電子彩色製版股份有限公司
印刷：錦龍印刷實業股份有限公司

發行者：黃淑惠
出版者：味全出版社有限公司
台北市仁愛路四段28號2樓
郵政劃撥0018203-8號　　黃淑惠帳戶
TEL:2702-1148.2702-1149
FAX:2704-2729

AUTHOR: Chen Shiu-Lee
COOKING ASSISTANT: Tsai Shou-Lien
EDITORIAL STAFF: Chiu Cheng-Tzu,
Chen Su-Jen, Chang Li-Wen
TRANSLATOR: Karen S. Chung

PHOTOGRAPHY: K. Lin
DESIGN: F. Chang

PRINTED IN TAIWAN, R.O.C.
Jin Long Printing & Stationery Co., Ltd.

WEI-CHUAN PUBLISHING
1455 Monterey Pass Rd., #110
Monterey Park, Ca 91754, U.S.A.
Tel: (323) 261-3880 · (323) 261-3878
Fax: (323) 261-3299

2nd Fl., 28 Section 4, Jen-Ai Road
Taipei, Taiwan, R.O.C.
Tel: (02) 2702-1148 · (02) 2702-1149
Fax: (02) 2704-2729

IRST PRINTING: DECEMBER 1988
10TH PRINTING: October 1998
ISBN 0-941676-19-6

序

十多年來優游於教學的領域中，對於各色烹飪之理論、技巧，多有心得。其中日本料理因其清淡不油膩的特性，深得我心，更精心鑽研。近年來國民生活水準日益提高，崇尚清淡、健康食品乃蔚為風尚，日本料理的特色正能符合此項需求。因此，在諸多烹飪界前輩，如黃淑惠教授、邱澄子女士等的鼓勵、提携之下，乃決定出版這本"日本料理"，以饗讀者。

為使本書內容更臻盡善盡美，兩年來，遍尋日本各地名師，如越野鶴松、宮崎幸枝、松本基子、落合輝惠、上野裕示和初田育穗等名教授切磋請益，實獲益良多，更使本書增色不少，在此特致上最誠摯的謝意。此外，我又將平日授課較具心得者，擇其具代表性而膾炙人口的菜餚，彙編而成本書，由淺入深、循序漸進，有適於大宴小酌的珍饈佳餚，也有簡便易作的一品料理。至於較特殊的調理技巧，其訣竅均詳列書中，相信讀者一定能很快掌握要訣，作出賞心怡人的精緻美食。關於日本料理所偏重的甜、酸之比重，我略作改變，以更適合國人的口味。此外，日本料理最講究精緻、美觀、氣氛及食器的選用，本書的精美圖片，可作為您享用日本料理的參考，讓著重高品味享受的您，能吃得美味、吃得健康，更吃得雅緻、吃出藝術。

承蒙映像攝影、七都里餐廳、名瓷公司及中興百貨等各界先進大力襄助，終能付梓。倉促成書，若有舛誤，尚祈海內外賢達不吝賜教。

陳綉麗 Chen Shiu-Lee.

DECEMBER 1988

INTRODUCTION

More than ten years of involvement in teaching about food have taught me much, particularly in the areas of different cooking principles and techniques. Of all the different cooking styles I have tried, I have a special fondness for Japanese cooking. What appeals most to me about it is that it is light, subtly flavored, and not oily; and for this reason I devoted myself to mastering its methods and techniques. With the rise in living standards, people have come to prefer light and healthful food, and Japanese food fills precisely these requirements. At the kind encouragement and guidance of several outstanding masters of cooking, such as Ms. Huang Su-Huei and Ms. Cheng-Tzu Chiu, I decided to put together this guide to JAPANESE CUISINE to share with you, our readers.

In preparation for this book, I visited several famous cooks in Japan, such as Tsurumatsu Koshino, Miaraki Yukie, Motoko Matsumoto, Terue Ojiai, Chiromi Ueno, and Ikuo Hatsuda, to solicit their opinions and discuss the various recipes. I learned much from all of them, and their knowledge and experience have greatly enriched this book. I offer here my sincerest and heartfelt thanks to each one. In addition, I have chosen some of the most representative and tastiest from among the dishes I teach in my cooking classes, and included them in this book. There are delicious and elegant dishes for formal banquets as well as for smaller meals, and easy-to-prepare one-dish meals. The book describes, step-by-step and in clear detail, all the special techniques and methods of Japanese cooking you need to master the preparation of each mouthwatering dish.

Japanese food frequently relies on a taste contrast between sweet and sour; I have toned these flavors down somewhat in this book to better adapt the dishes to non-Japanese preferences. One important feature of Japanese food is its delicacy, elegant presentation, atmosphere, and choice of utensils. The colorful photographs in this book can be your guide to preparing and serving artistic feasts for all the senses.

This book owes its existence to the enormous assistance provided by K. Lin Studio, Natori Restaurant, Mine Tryz Trading Company, and Sunrise Department Store. We sincerely hope our readers living in all parts of the globe will kindly offer their criticisms and suggestions to help us improve future editions.

目錄 TABLE OF CONTENTS

重量換算表（本書重量單位採公制，讀者可依下表換算使用。）

公克	37.5	75	150	225	300	375	450	600
兩	1	2	4	6	8	10	12	16

日本料理
特殊調味品

1 濃口、淡口醬油由黃豆、麥、米等釀製而成。濃口即一般傳統醬油。淡口顏色較淡，內含果糖，多使用於淡色菜中。

2 煮出汁（ほんだし）分顆粒狀、液狀，有柴魚汁、海帶汁、小魚乾汁等多種口味，可代替中國菜的高湯使用。

3 味醂（みりん）用糯米釀製而成，色透明、味甜之液體，爲日本料理常用調味料之一。

4 海苔香鬆（ふりかけ）常用以拌飯或做壽司，是用芝麻、海苔、柴魚等製成，種類多，可任選。

5 味噌醬用黃豆及米、麥等醱酵釀製而成，分鹹味、淡味。

6 芥茉醬（からし）爲芥菜籽磨成粉所做成的膏狀調味料，色黃味辣。

7 山葵醬（わさひ）係山葵的根、莖磨成粉所做成的膏狀調味料，色綠味辣。

8 七味辣粉爲青紫蘇、花椒、小茴香、三奈、芝麻、辣椒、胡椒粒等多種香料炒香後製成。

SPECIAL SEASONING INGREDIENTS USED IN JAPANESE COOKING

1 **Dark and Light Soy Sauce (*Shōyu*)** Soy sauce is brewed from soy beans, wheat, rice, and other ingredients. Dark soy sauce is the most common kind; light-colored soy sauce contains fructose, and is often used in light-colored dishes.

2 **Dashi** *Dashi* base comes in either powdered or liquid form, and in bonito, kelp, and small dried fish flavors. Use *dashi* as stock in cooking.

3 **Mirin** *Mirin* is a transparent, sweet cooking wine made from glutinous rice, frequently used in Japanese cooking.

4 **Crushed Laver (*Furigake*)** This condiment, containing sesame seeds, finely crushed purple laver (*nori*), and bits of dried bonito fillet, comes in many different types, and is usually mixed into rice or used in making *sushi*. Use the type you prefer.

5 **Miso (Soy Bean Paste)** *Miso* is made of soy beans, rice, wheat, and other ingredients. It comes in regular and low-salt types.

6 **Mustard** This is a yellow, piquant paste made from mustard seed powder.

7 **Wasabi (Japanese Horseradish)** Japanese horseradish root is first ground into a powder, then made into a green, piquant paste.

8 **Seven-Flavor Seasoning (*Shichimi-tōgarashi*)** This seasoning is made from toasted white radish sprouts, Szechuan peppercorns, fennel, pepper leaf, sesame seed, chili pepper, and pepper.

1

5

2

6

3

7

4

8

煮出汁
基本做法

在日本料理中，煮出汁佔了一席重要之地，一道菜的鮮美與否，經常取決於煮出汁的好壞。煮出汁可分爲煮出汁(一)、煮出汁(二)，其做法如下：

煮出汁(一)

鰹(柴)魚片(圖１)⋯⋯⋯⋯⋯⋯⋯20～30公克
水⋯⋯⋯⋯⋯⋯⋯⋯⋯⋯⋯⋯⋯5杯
乾海帶(圖２)⋯⋯⋯⋯⋯⋯⋯⋯1條(10公分)

■乾海帶用布擦乾淨後攤開，每隔約１公分處剪開成長條狀，但不能剪斷，可使鮮味易出且撈取方便。

■鍋內入水５杯及海帶，中火煮至沸騰前將海帶取出，續煮開隨入鰹魚片立即熄火，待鰹魚片沈澱後，再以紗布過濾即成，可使用於淡色菜中，如茶碗蒸等。
□整塊的鰹魚可先烤軟再刨薄片。

煮出汁(二)

將煮出汁(一)中已煮過一次的海帶及鰹魚片，加水２½杯，中火再煮至沸騰前，再加入鰹魚片20公克立即熄火，待沈澱後過濾即成，可使用於濃色菜中如筑前煮等。
□市售現成的煮出汁(圖３)使用更方便。

HOW TO MAKE DASHI STOCK

Dashi stock plays an important role in Japanese cooking. The freshness and tastiness of a dish often depend to a great extent on the quality of the *dashi* used. Presented below are methods for making the two different kinds of *dashi*:

Dashi I

2/3 to 1 oz. (20-30 g) dried bonito shavings (*katsuobushi*; illus. 1)
5 c. water
1 strip (4″ or 10 cm) dried kelp seaweed (*kombu*; illus. 2)

■ Rub the kelp clean with a cloth, then spread open. Make a series of cuts in the kelp crosswise at 1/2″ (1 cm) intervals; do not, however, cut all the way through. These cuts allow the kelp to release more of its flavor into the stock while cooking; and leaving the kelp in one piece makes it easy to remove.
■ Add the 5 cups of water to a pot together with the kelp. Before the center begins to boil, remove the kelp and continue to boil. Add the bonito shavings and turn off the heat immediately. After the bonito shavings have settled to the bottom of the pot, filter the stock through a piece of cheesecloth. The *dashi* stock is now ready for use in light-colored dishes, for example, Savory Cup Custard (Chawan Mushi; p. 39).
□ Whole dried bonito fillets may be baked to soften and shaved to make the bonito shavings.

Dashi II

Add 2-1/2 cups water to the kelp and bonito shavings used in Dashi I and heat in a pot. Before the center begins to boil, add another 2/3 oz. (20 g) of bonito shavings and turn off the heat immediately. Wait until the ingredients have settled, and filter through a piece of cheesecloth. This *dashi* can be used in dishes with a darker color, such as Chikuzen Ni (p.24). Use ready-made *dashi* for extra convenience (illus. 3).

1

2

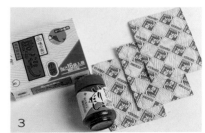

3

壽司飯做法

壽司飯（４人份）

選擇米粒精白無雜質且碎米少之蓬萊米或壽司米２杯洗淨（米切忌搓洗過度，以免維他命Ｂ₁流失），視其色潔白透明即可瀝乾水份，並加水１¾杯浸泡３０分鐘以上，用電鍋（或瓦斯）將米煮熟後續燜約１５分鐘趁熱淋上壽司醋，用飯杓由下往上翻拌，並以扇子（或電扇）邊搧邊拌，將飯粒翻鬆，並將醋的酸味吹散（圖１）。飯粒不能成糰亦不能壓緊，否則會有黏性（圖２），即為壽司飯。

□ 拌好的壽司飯如量多，宜移入另一容器內，蓋上溼布以免乾硬且容易保存，但家庭做量少可免。

壽司醋做法

將白醋３大匙及塩½小匙以小火煮開，並加白砂糖２大匙後立即熄火，待糖完全溶化即成。壽司醋須預先煮好備用，因此可一次多做些存放冰箱，方便取用。糖與醋的比例可隨個人喜愛增減，市售各種不同品牌的壽司醋亦可任意選用（圖３）。

拌飯器具

選用底面積大而平的木製容器較能吸收蒸氣、水份，使米粒更光亮而富有彈性。如無，可以瓷器或不銹鋼容器代替。

□ 木製容器保存方法：
使用後速洗淨，風乾水份（不能曬太陽）存放陰涼處下次使用前再用乾布擦乾淨即可。

HOW TO MAKE RICE FOR SUSHI

Sushi rice (serves 4)

Choose short-grain or *sushi* rice that has whole, pure white grains, with no foreign material mixed in, and with a minimum of broken grains. Wash 2 cups of the rice (do not wash and rinse too long, so as to avoid losing the vitamin B_1 content in the rice). Drain when the rice is clean, white, and translucent. Add 1-3/4 cups water and soak 30 minutes or longer. Cook in an electric rice cooker (or on an electric or gas stove) until done. Leave the rice covered and undisturbed for another 15 minutes after turning off the heat. Pour the *sushi* vinegar over the cooked rice while the rice is still hot, and mix it in with a rice paddle. Fan the rice (either by hand or with an electric fan) while mixing in the vinegar. Do this until the rice is light and fluffy, and the flavor of the vinegar dispersed (illus. 1). Do not allow the rice grains to cling together in clumps, and do not squish the grains, or the rice will become sticky and pasty (illus. 2).

□ If you make a large quantity of *sushi* rice, transfer the extra rice to another container and cover with a wet cloth to prevent the rice from becoming dry and hard. This step is not necessary if making only a small amount for home use.

Sushi vinegar

Mix 1/2 teaspoon salt into 3 tablespoons rice vinegar and bring to a boil over low heat. Then add 2 tablespoons granulated white sugar and turn off the heat immediately. The vinegar mixture is ready when the sugar has completely dissolved. *Sushi* vinegar must be prepared ahead of time, so it is convenient to make a large amount at once and keep it in the refrigerator for use when necessary. The proportion of sugar to vinegar can be adjusted according to personal taste. The various brands of *sushi* vinegar available commercially may also be used (illus. 3).

Utensils for mixing the sushi rice

A wooden container with a large, flat bottom can absorb steam and moisture, allowing the rice grains to become springy and glossy. If unavailable, a porcelain or stainless steel container may be substituted.

□ How to store wooden containers
Wash immediately after use, and drip-dry (do not dry in the sun). Store in a dark, cool, and dry place. Wipe clean with a dry cloth before the next use.

1

2

3

自製烏龍麵　4-5人份

水 ……………………………130c.c.(約½杯)
塩 ……………………………10公克(約½大匙)
低筋麵粉 ……………………200公克(約⅔杯)
高筋麵粉 ……………………100公克(約⅓杯)
乾麵粉(低筋) …………………………¼杯

■ 將水及塩混合溶化成與海水一樣的鹹度，或用量塩器量至15度(圖１)。

■ 盆內放入低筋麵粉及高筋麵粉混合，並徐徐加入塩水攪拌均勻，蓋上溼布醒約１小時後取出，以手掌心壓按(圖２)後，再摺三褶繼續壓按，依此動作反覆做５分鐘(約３～４次)。

■ 醒過的麵糰置台上，揉至軟硬適中的程度，再醒20分鐘，取出用擀麵桿擀成10公分×20公分之長方形麵皮，並撒少許乾麵粉，用擀麵桿將麵皮卷起(圖３)，邊擀邊壓，使麵皮拉長，再將麵皮攤開，撒乾麵粉少許後，再卷起麵皮，如此反覆做５次以上，至麵皮厚約0.2公分，撒上多量乾麵粉摺成３～４層，用刀切成0.3公分寬的烏龍麵，再撒多量乾麵粉即成。

□ 自製烏龍麵較富彈性，可炒可煮，非常方便，如不馬上煮，可以保鮮膜包好存放冰箱，約可保存一星期。

□ 餐館製作份量多可將麵糰先用塑膠袋套好，並放上一塊墊布，再以雙腳踩踏代替手掌壓按，使麵筋鬆弛。

烏龍麵煮法

水燒開，放入烏龍麵煮滾，再加１杯冷水，續煮約１分鐘，視麵心熟透，撈出漂涼瀝乾水份即可。

HOW TO MAKE HOMEMADE UDON NOODLES

SERVES 4-5

1/2 c. (130 cc) water
1/2 T. (10 g) salt
7 oz. (200 g) low gluten flour (about 2/3 c.)
3-1/2 oz. (100 g) high gluten flour (about 1/3 c.)
1/4 c. low gluten flour

■ Dissolve the salt in the water. It should be about as salty as sea water (15 units on a salinometer; illus. 1).

■ Mix the low gluten flour and high gluten flour together in a large bowl. Add the salt water very slowly to the flour as you knead it into a smooth dough. Cover with a wet cloth and leave undisturbed for about one hour. Remove from the bowl. Press the dough down with the palm of your hand (illus. 2), fold into three parts, then press down again. Repeat the above steps for 5 minutes (about 3 to 4 times).

■ Place the dough on a counter and knead until of a consistency that is neither too soft nor too firm. Allow to set undisturbed for another 20 minutes. Remove from the bowl and use a rolling pin (preferably one with about the same diameter as a broomstick) to roll out into a 4″×8″ (10×20 cm) rectangle. Sprinkle some flour over the top. Roll up the dough on the rolling pin (illus. 3) to flatten. You will be rolling out several separate looped layers at once. Press down and roll to lengthen the dough. Spread open the dough on the counter, sprinkle some flour over it, and again roll up the dough around the rolling pin. Repeat as above 5 more times until the dough is about 1/12″ (.2 cm) thick. Sprinkle liberally with flour and fold into 3 or 4 layers. Cut into 1/8″ (.3 cm) *udon* noodles. Again sprinkle liberally with flour, and the noodles are ready for use.

□ Homemade *udon* noodles have a pleasantly springy texture. They can be either stir-fried or boiled, and are very convenient to use. If you do not use them immediately after making them, wrap them in plastic and keep in the refrigerator. They will stay fresh for about one week.

□ For restaurants that make *udon* noodles in large quantities, the dough can be placed in a plastic bag, and a piece of cloth spread on top of the bag. The dough is then stamped on with the feet, rather than kneaded by hand. This makes the gluten in the flour soft and pliable.

To cook *udon* noodles:

Fill a pot with water and bring to a boil. Add the *udon* and wait until the water comes to a second boil. Add 1 cup of cold water, then cook another minute. Remove the noodles when cooked through, and rinse in cold water.

3

1

2

魚類處理方法

■魚爲日本料理的主菜之一，尤以生魚片爲然，因此如何選購魚類益形重要。做生魚片所使用的魚類首重新鮮，亦即要選購眼部明亮清澈，色澤鮮艷亮麗，魚肉晶瑩剔透而有彈性的新鮮魚或活魚，通常以海水魚類爲主（因淡水魚很少生吃），冷藏溫度須隨時保持３℃至５℃之間，以免魚肉變質（但不得低於３℃以免結凍）。所使用的砧板、刀、白毛巾等更應隨時保持清潔。

魚洗淨，去除內臟，再以冷開水沖洗乾淨，剔骨取肉切片後便不能再沖洗了，否則鮮味會流失且易腐爛。剔魚骨取肉的刀工，在做生魚片的步驟中，佔極重要的一環，讀者祇要參照分解圖反覆練習，很快就能掌握要訣。謹將剔魚骨的基本方法及握壽司生魚片的切法分別解析如下：

NOTES ON FISH IN JAPANESE COOKING

■ Fish is one of the mainstays of the Japanese diet, especially in the form of *sashimi* (cut raw fish). It is thus extremely important to know how to select fish. Freshness is by far the top priority: choose fresh or live fish with bright and clear eyes, and translucent, firm, springy flesh. Salt water fish are the most commonly used (fresh water fish are seldom eaten raw). The fish must be kept at a temperature between 37.4°F (3°C) and 41°F (5°C) to prevent spoilage. (Do not, however, let the temperature fall below 37.4°F (3°C), or the fish will freeze.) It is also important to keep the cutting board,

knife, white towels, etc. used in preparing *sashimi* clean. Wash the fish, remove the entrails, then rinse again in cold water. The fish cannot be rinsed once it has been deboned, since contact with water would wash away the flavor, and also make it more vulnerable to rapid spoilage.

Learning to debone fish is a key step in making *sashimi*. You need only refer to the illustrations below and practice several times to master this procedure. Illustrated and explained below are the methods for deboning fish and for preparing fish for pressed *sushi* with *sashimi*.

(一)剔魚骨的基本方法 (圖 1～12) Basic Method for Deboning Fish (illus. 1-12)

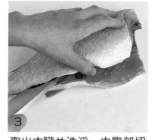
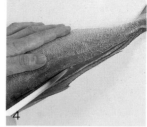

由魚鰭旁下刀，刀面略向左斜，觸及大骨，反面亦同，切下魚頭。

刀由下腹切入，由左向右切到底。

取出內臟並洗淨，由腹部切向魚尾。

再由背鰭上方下刀，觸及大骨，由右至左切到底。

Start cutting near the fins. Hold the knife slightly angled to the left. When you cut down to the large bone, turn the fish over, repeat this same cut, and remove the head.

Insert the knife below the belly and cut from left to right, all the way through.

Remove the entrails and wash the fish. Cut from the belly to the tail.

Next, cut from the upper back fin area down. When you hit the main bone, cut from right to left, all the way through.

5

刀串入尾部，朝頭部方向下刀，觸及大骨取肉。

Insert the knife into the tail portion and cut, down to the bone, towards the head. Remove the fillet.

6

切下尾部相連部份，便可取下一邊的魚肉。

Cut into the area where the tail is joined. You can now remove the fillet from one side.

7

另一邊魚肉剔法相同，切好即成三片。

Follow the same procedure to remove the fillet from the other side. When correctly sliced, it will come off in three pieces.

8

剔下腹部魚刺，另一邊剔法相同。

Cut off the fish bones from the belly. Repeat on the other side.

9

由肉與皮之間下刀，左手拉緊魚皮，以推刀方式取肉。

Insert a knife between the flesh and the skin. Grasp the skin with your left hand. Remove the flesh by pushing the knife in.

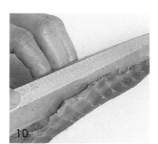

10

將背腹間或深色魚肉處的小刺切除(或用夾子拔出)。

Cut off the small bones in the posterior ventral area, where the dark-colored meat is (or remove the bones with a tweezers).

11

修成等邊的長方塊(似木塊形)。

Trim the flesh into a rectangle (so that it resembles a block of wood).

12

用生魚片刀，直刀切下即為平片造型。

Cut with a *sashimi* knife as illustrated to form flat slices.

(二)握壽司生魚片切法 (圖13～16) Preparing Sashimi for Pressed Sushi (illus. 13-16)

13

鮪魚腹部(卜口)的肉有油質最滑嫩可口。

The belly flesh of tuna fish has a high fat content, and is the most tender and delicious part of the fish.

14

逆紋斜切約0.3公分薄片(刀鋒向左斜，一刀切斷)。

Cut into slices about 1/8" (.3 cm) thick at an angle against the grain (angle the knife to the left, and cut each slice off with one stroke of the knife).

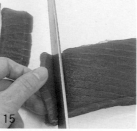

15

背部也逆紋直刀切約0.3公分薄片(刀鋒略偏右，切出圓弧狀)。

Again, cut the back portion into 1/8" (.3 cm) thick slices at an angle against the grain (the knife tip should be angled somewhat to the right, then angled back, so the slices have a rounded edge).

16

圓弧狀魚片較立體方便擺飾

Slices with a rounded edge give a three-dimensional effect and are convenient for use in arrangements.

實用全餐舉例
實用献立

日本料理以講求器皿的擺飾及氣氛的搭配爲重,至於菜餚的選擇主要爲三菜一湯,即一道主菜(如生魚片、烤物、煎肉或酥炸海鮮等),二道副菜,以簡易而不與主菜重複爲原則,一道湯(清湯、濃湯或味噌湯均可),一碟泡菜,一碗飯即可。茲舉一例(如圖)供讀者參考:

主菜　綜合生魚片(參考第12頁)。
副菜　芝麻牛肉(做法如右)。
　　　鮮魚蒸豆腐(參考第42頁)。
湯　　味噌湯(參考第18頁)。
醃菜　醃黃蘿蔔或醃白菜(參考51頁)。
飯　　通常以白飯撒少許芝麻即可,節慶時可改用什錦飯(參考第88頁)或紅豆飯(參考第85頁)替代。

芝麻牛肉
牛肉のごま風味焼　　　　　　　4人份

牛里肌肉	‧‧‧‧‧‧	400公克
1	醬油	2大匙
	酒	¼杯
	味醂	2大匙
	白芝麻(炒好)	1½大匙
青花菜(煮熟)	‧‧‧‧‧‧	適量
紅蘿蔔(煮熟)	‧‧‧‧‧‧	適量

■牛肉切薄片醃1料約30分鐘。
■平底鍋燒熱,加油1大匙,將肉片快炒約八分熟,盛入容器,旁置青花菜及紅蘿蔔即成。

EXAMPLE OF A COMPLETE JAPANESE MEAL

In a formal Japanese dinner, the arrangement of the utensils and the atmosphere they create are central to the meal. The meal itself usually consists of three entrees and a soup: one main dish (for example, *sashimi*, a broiled food, a fried meat dish, batter-fried seafood, etc.), two side dishes (as a rule, these are simpler dishes that do not repeat ingredients used in the main dish), soup (consommé, thick soup, or miso soup), a dish of pickled vegetables, and a bowl of rice. Here is an example of a complete Japanese style meal as a reference:

Main Dish: Assorted Sashimi (see p. 12).
Side Dishes: Sesame Beef (recipe right); Fresh Fish Steamed with Tofu (see p. 42).
Soup: Miso Soup (see p. 18).
Pickle: Yellow Pickled Radish (*Takuan*) or Pickled Cabbage (see p. 51).
Rice: Usually white rice with some sesame seeds sprinkled over the top is served; on special occasions, Little-of-Everything Rice (see p. 88) or Red Bean Rice (see p. 85) can be substituted.

SESAME BEEF
SERVES 4

1	7/8 lb. (400 g) lean beef
	2 T. soy sauce
	1/4 c. rice wine
	2 T. *mirin* (sweet rice wine)
	1-1/2 T. white sesame seeds (toasted)

cooked broccoli, as desired
cooked carrot, as desired

■ Cut the beef into thin slices and marinate in 1 about 30 minutes.
■ Heat a flat-bottomed frying pan, add 1 tablespoon oil, and stir-fry the beef rapidly until medium-well done. Transfer to a serving dish. Place some cooked broccoli and carrot on the side and serve.

本料理由七都里餐廳提供

綜合生魚片
お造り盛り合わせ　　　　4人份

鮪魚肉··································180公克
鯛魚肉··································300公克
花枝··································150公克
紫菜····································1張
水針魚肉(長8公分)························1條
小黃瓜····································1條
鳥貝····································4片
血蚶····································2個
白蘿蔔絲·································¼杯
山葵醬、醬油·····························適量

■鮪魚肉切成1公分厚長條，鯛魚肉切0.5公分厚斜片備用。
■花枝去頭、內臟、表皮及膜(圖1)切對半，取一片在肉面橫切一刀，不能切斷(圖2)內側夾上一張紫菜(圖3)，切0.7公分寬條，另一片切薄片捲花(參考"拼盤與盤飾"第103頁)。
■水針魚肉捲上小黃瓜切塊，鳥貝及血蚶(切花刀)分別洗淨備用。
■白蘿蔔絲泡冰水約30分鐘，使用前瀝乾水份。
■將材料分別整齊排在容器上，沾山葵醬、醬油食用。
□魚肉切的好壞是生魚片中的一門學問，主要是刀要利，一刀切下使切口如大理石般的平滑。切好魚肉應貯存冰箱，溫度需在3℃至5℃之間，最好當天食用，若有剩餘，宜煮熟食用。
□如無水針魚可以其他新鮮海水魚類代替。

ASSORTED SASHIMI
SERVES 4

6-1/2 oz. (180 g) fresh tuna fish fillet
　(*maguro*)
2/3 lb. (300 g) porgy (red sea bream;
　tai)
1/3 lb. (150 g) fresh cuttlefish or squid
　(*ika*)
1 sheet purple laver seaweed (*nori*)
1 halfbeak fish (*sayori*) (3″ or 8 cm long)
1 small gherkin cucumber
4 cockles (*torigai*)
2 ark shells (*akagai*)
1/4 c. shredded Chinese white radish
　(*daikon*)
wasabi (Japanese horseradish) and soy
　sauce, as desired

■ Slice the tuna into 3/8″ (1 cm) thick strips. Cut the porgy into 1/8″ (.5 cm) thick diagonally-cut slices. Set aside.
■ Remove the head, entrails, outer skin, and membrane from the cuttlefish (illus. 1). Cut in half lengthwise. Make a horizontal slash in one of the pieces on the interior; do not cut all the way through (illus. 2). Insert a sheet of *nori* inside (illus. 3), and cut into 3/8″ (1 cm) wide strips. Cut the other half of the cuttlefish into thin slices, and roll into flowers (see page 103 of ''Chinese Appetizers and Garnishes'').
■ Roll the gherkin cucumber inside the halfbeak fish fillet. Cut into pieces. Score the cockles and ark shells (with a crosshatch cut), wash each separately, and set aside.
■ Soak the shredded white radish in ice water about 30 minutes. Drain well before using.
■ Neatly arrange the ingredients separately on a serving dish. Dip in a mixture of *wasabi* and soy sauce to eat.
□ Cutting *sashimi* is an art; the important things to remember are that the knife should be sharp, each cut should be made in a single stroke, and the resulting piece of fish should be as smooth as a piece of marble. *Sashimi* should be stored in the refrigerator at a temperature between 37.4° and 41°F (3° to 5°C), and is best if eaten the same day it is prepared. If there are leftovers, it is best to serve them cooked rather than raw.
□ If halfbeak fish is unavailable, substitute any other fresh salt water fish.

本料理由七都里餐廳提供

1

2

3

生鮮蝦片

車えびのあらい　　　4人份

活明蝦（約10～12公分）	…………	4 條
檸檬	…………	1 個
青紫蘇葉（圖1）	…………	4 葉
山葵醬	…………	適量
	醋	3 大匙
1	開水	1½ 大匙
	醬油	1½ 大匙

■明蝦洗淨將蝦頭放入開水中略煮，見色轉紅撈起，浸冰水。檸檬半個切圓薄片，另半個切四等份。

■蝦身去殼，蝦背直劃2～3刀，不能切斷（圖2）。盆內置冰塊及冰水，放入蝦肉，用筷子或湯匙反覆攪打1分鐘（圖3），至蝦肉緊縮捲起呈脆硬狀。

■取碎冰塊置容器，放入檸檬片，上置蝦肉及山葵醬，食用時沾上1料。另將青紫蘇葉、蝦頭及檸檬塊置小碟，亦可同時使用。

□可將青紫蘇葉包捲蝦肉而食，亦別具風味。

□如無青紫蘇葉，亦可以巴西利代替。

FRESH SHRIMP APPETIZER

SERVES 4

4 live prawns (about 4 to 4-3/4″
    or 10 to 12 cm)
1 lemon
4 plum leaves (*ōba*; illus. 1)
wasabi (Japanese horseradish),
    as desired

1 | 3 T. rice vinegar
  | 1-1/2 T. water
  | 1-1/2 T. soy sauce

■ Wash the prawns. Remove the heads and blanch in boiling water. Remove as soon as they turn red in color, then soak in ice water. Cut half of the lemon into thin rounds, and quarter the other half.

■ Shell the shrimp and make 2 to 3 slashes down the back of each; do not cut all the way through (illus. 2). Fill a bowl with ice water and ice cubes, then add the shrimp. Stir the shrimp around in the ice water with a pair of chopsticks or a spoon for 1 minute (illus. 3), until the flesh of the shrimp becomes firm, and it shrinks and curls up.

■ Place some crushed ice in a serving bowl, then top with the lemon rounds. On top of this place the shrimp and the *wasabi*. Dip in 1 to eat. Place the plum leaves, the shrimp heads, and the quartered half lemon on a small dish and serve on the side.

□ The shrimp can be wrapped in the plum leaves before eating for variety.

□ If plum leaves are unavailable, parsley may be used as a substitute.

本料理由七都里餐廳提供

1

2

3

生鮮牛肉

牛肉のたたつき　　　4人份

嫩牛肉(或腓脷)		450公克
1	白蘿蔔	½條
	紅辣椒	½條
葱		2枝
洋葱		½個
蒜		2粒
2	檸檬汁	1大匙
	醬油	1大匙
	煮出汁	½杯

■選擇肉質鮮紅有彈性的嫩牛肉，去除筋、油(圖1)，逆紋切薄片(圖2)排盤，用保鮮膜包好(圖3)，置冰箱冰約2小時(溫度約為3℃至5℃)。

■將1料磨泥(參考第42頁鮮魚蒸豆腐)，葱切細末，洋葱切絲浸冰水約10分鐘，使用時瀝乾水份，蒜磨成細泥，將全部材料撒在冰涼的牛肉片上，食時淋上拌勻的2料即可。

□選購生食牛肉以新鮮為主，冷藏溫度須保持3℃～5℃之間，冰約6天以上，肉質更鮮嫩。

□亦可將配料全部磨成泥，拌上鮮蛋黃、醬油及麻油又是另一種風味。

FRESH BEEF APPETIZER

SERVES 4

	1 lb. (450 g) tender lean beef (or fillet)	
1	1/2 Chinese white radish (*daikon*)	
	1/2 small red chili pepper	
	2 green onions	
	1/2 onion	
	2 cloves garlic	
2	1 T. lemon juice	
	1 T. soy sauce	
	1/2 c. *dashi*	

■ Choose tender lean beef that is bright red and springy to the touch. Trim off the sinews and fat (illus. 1). Cut against the grain into thin slices (illus. 2), and arrange on a plate. Cover and seal with plastic wrap (illus. 3). Refrigerate 2 hours (at 37.4° to 41°F or 3° to 5 °C).

■ Grind 1 into a puree (see p. 42, Fresh Fish Steamed with Tofu), mince the green onion finely, and cut the onion into half rings. Soak the onion in ice water about 10 minutes. Drain well before using. Puree the garlic. Sprinkle all of the ingredients over the cold beef. To serve, mix 2 well and pour over the beef.

□ When choosing beef that is to be eaten raw, freshness is of the utmost importance. The beef should be refrigerated at a temperature of 37.4° to 41°F (3° to 5°C). For tastier and more tender beef, refrigerate for 6 days or more.

□ The dressing ingredients may, as an alternative, be pureed together, then mixed well with fresh raw egg yolk, soy sauce, and sesame oil.

味噌湯

みそ汁　　　4人份

■鯛骨（或其他新鮮魚骨）切塊（圖２），入開水川燙撈出，再用清水洗淨。
■鍋內入水３½杯燒開，將紅、白蘿蔔絲煮軟，續入魚骨煮滾，去除泡沫，將１料置小漏杓內，以木棍（或湯匙）拌勻（圖３），立即熄火盛碗，並撒上葱花即成。
□若將魚骨改用豆腐、海帶芽，水則改用魚干汁（小魚干300公克去頭及內臟，加水５杯以小火煮20分鐘即成）較理想。

鯛骨（赤鯮魚骨）…………………………	300公克
紅、白蘿蔔絲……………………………	各½杯
味噌（圖１）……………………………	80公克
糖、味精…………………………………	各⅛小匙
葱花………………………………………	２大匙

MISO SOUP

SERVES 4

■ Cut the porgy (or other fresh fish) bones into pieces (illus. 2). Blanch briefly in boiling water, remove, and rinse under the tap.
■ Put 3-1/2 cups water into a pot and bring to a boil. Add the shredded *daikon* and carrot and cook until soft. Next add the fish bones and bring the soup to a boil. Skim off the foam. Pass 1 through a spoon sieve. Mix thoroughly with a wooden stick or a spoon (illus. 3). Turn off the heat immediately and pour the soup into a serving bowl. Sprinkle some chopped green onion over the top and serve.
□ *Tofu* and *wakame* (lobe-leaf seaweed) may be substituted for the fish bones, and dried fish broth for the water. (Remove the heads and entrails from 2/3 lb or 300g small dried fish. Add 5 cups water and cook over low heat for 20 minutes.)

- 2/3 lb. (300g) porgy (red sea bream; *tai*)
- 1/2 c. each: shredded *daikon*, shredded carrot
- 1-2/3 oz. (80 g) *miso* (soy bean paste; illus. 1)
- 1/8 t. each: sugar, MSG (optional)
- 2 T. chopped green onion

明蝦湯

車えびの吸物　　　4人份

明蝦4條…………………………150公克	
菠菜（燙熟）………………………少許	
魚板……………………………4片	
檸檬皮絲…………………………少許	
1 煮出汁………………………3½杯	
塩、醬油…………………各⅛小匙	

■蝦身去殼（圖1）背部劃直刀但不切斷（圖2），中間再劃一切口約1公分，尾端從切口處翻捲出形狀（圖3），放入開水內川燙約1分鐘撈出。

■將明蝦、菠菜、魚板及檸檬皮絲置碗，注入煮開的1料約七分滿即成。

□如無菠菜亦可用貝芽菜代替。

PRAWN SOUP

SERVES 4

4 prawns (1/3 lb. or 150 g)
small amount of fresh spinach,
  washed well and blanched in
  boiling water
4 slices fish cake (*kamaboko*)
small amount of shredded lemon
  peel
1 | 3-1/2 c. *dashi*
  | 1/8 t. each: salt, soy sauce

■ Remove the shell from the body of the shrimp (illus. 1). Slash the back vertically, but do not cut all the way through (illus. 2). Cut a notch in the center, about 3/8″ (1 cm) long. Pull the tail out from the notch and curl as illustrated (illus. 3). Blanch in boiling water for about one minute and remove.

■ Place the prawns, spinach, fish cake slices, and shredded lemon peel in a serving bowl. Bring 1 to a boil and pour into the bowl so it is about 7/10 full. Serve.

□ If spinach is unavailable, white radish sprouts (*kaiware*) may be substituted.

福袋煮

ふくぶくろに　　　4人份

■油豆腐皮切去一邊(圖1)，放入開水煮1分鐘(去除油腥)後撈出以冷水漂涼並擠乾水份。

■1料置鍋加2料煮約3分鐘後撈起，即爲餡。餘汁再放入油豆腐皮續煮約2分鐘取出待涼，汁留用。

■將豆腐皮切口打開，放入餡及湯汁(圖2)，袋口並用干瓢繫緊(圖3)即爲福袋。

■鍋內入3料、福袋及香菇燒開後，改小火續煮至汁剩1杯時，加豌豆略煮即成。

■容器內依序放入福袋、香菇及豌豆，並淋上少許餘汁，上擺薑絲即成，此道菜野餐或便當均適宜。

油豆腐皮(四方形)	·······8張	
1	雞肉絲······60公克、紅蘿蔔絲···30公克	
	筍絲······30公克、牛蒡絲······40公克	
	蒟蒻絲(川燙過)······80公克	
2	砂糖······3大匙、醬油······2大匙	
	塩······⅛小匙、煮出汁······½杯	
干瓢(20公分長，泡軟)······8條		
3	煮出汁······3杯、塩······⅛小匙	
	砂糖、醬油······各4大匙	
香菇(泡軟)······4朵、豌豆······8片		
薑絲······1大匙		

STUFFED TOFU POCKETS

SERVES 4

■ Cut off one edge from each of the fried *tofu* pockets (illus. 1). Immerse in boiling water 1 minute to remove the oily odor. Cool by placing in a bowl of cold water. Remove and squeeze out the excess moisture.

■ Add 1 and 2 to a pot, cook about 3 minutes, and remove. This is the filling for the *tofu* pockets. Place the fried *tofu* pockets in the remaining liquid and cook 2 minutes. Remove and cool. Save the liquid.

■ Open the fried *tofu* pockets and stuff each with some of the filling and sauce (illus. 2). Tie the opening shut with a dried gourd shaving, securing it tightly (illus. 3).

■ Add 3, the pockets, and the mushrooms to a pot and bring to a boil. Lower the heat and cook until the liquid is reduced to one cup. Add the Chinese peapods and cook briefly.

■ Arrange the pockets, mushrooms, and peapods on a serving dish, and pour the remaining liquid over the top. Serve with shredded ginger root.

☐ This dish is especially good for picnics and box lunches.

	8 square fried *tofu* pockets
	2 oz. (60 g) shredded chicken
	1 oz. (30 g) each: julienned carrot, julienned bamboo shoots.
1	1-1/3 oz. (40 g) julienned burdock root (*gobō*)
	2-2/3 oz. (80 g) *shirataki* (clear noodles made from devil's tongue paste), blanched in boiling water
2	3 T. sugar, 2 T. soy sauce
	1/8 t. salt, 1/2 c. *dashi*
	8 dried gourd shavings (*kampyō*), 8" (20 cm) each (soaked until soft; see p.69 Basic Rolled Sushi)
3	3 c. *dashi*, 1/8 t. salt
	4 T. each: sugar, soy sauce
	4 dried Chinese black mushrooms (*shiitake*; soaked until soft)
	8 Chinese peapods
	1 T. shredded ginger root

南瓜鷄米

かぼちやのそぼろあんかけ　　　4人份

南瓜1個	··········	500公克
雞胸肉	··········	80公克
1	煮出汁	2杯
	糖	2大匙
	味醂	3大匙
	淡口醬油	2大匙
2	太白粉	1小匙
	水	1½小匙
薑絲	··········	1大匙

■南瓜（圖1）切半去籽（圖2）每間隔1公分去皮（圖3）切塊。雞胸肉去皮剁碎。
■鍋內入1料及南瓜以小火煮至熟透（約15分鐘）盛出，一片片排列整齊，汁留用。
■鍋熱加油1小匙，炒香雞米，入南瓜汁燒開，再以2料勾芡，淋於南瓜上，上置薑絲即成。
□南瓜以選肉質較厚者為佳。

PUMPKIN WITH CHICKEN

SERVES 4

1 pumpkin (1 lb. 2 oz. or 500 g)
2-2/3 oz. (80 g) chicken breast fillet

1
2 c. *dashi*
2 T. sugar
3 T. *mirin* (sweet rice wine)
2 T. light-colored soy sauce

2
1 t. cornstarch
1-1/2 t. water

1 T. shredded ginger root

■ Cut the pumpkin (illus. 1) in half and remove the seeds (illus. 2). Remove the skin at 3/8″ (1 cm) intervals (illus. 3) and cut into chunks. Remove the skin from the chicken breast fillet and chop the meat finely.
■ Add 1 and the pumpkin chunks to a pot and cook over low heat until completely done (about 15 minutes). Remove from the broth, and arrange in neat rows on a serving dish. Save the broth.
■ Heat a frying pan, add 1 teaspoon oil, and stir-fry the chopped chicken. Add the liquid from cooking the pumpkin and bring to a boil. Thicken with 2, and pour over the pumpkin. Top with shredded ginger root, and serve.
□ Pumpkins with thick flesh are best for this recipe.

煮金線魚

いとよりの煮つけ　4人份

金線魚	·····	600公克
1	煮出汁	·····	1 杯
	酒	·····	⅔杯
	糖	·····	2 大匙
	淡口醬油	·····	½杯
金菇	·····	200公克
豌豆	·····	6 片
紅、白蘿蔔絲	·····	共 1¼杯
檸檬	·····	¼個

■金線魚由背部上方割一刀，觸及大骨，反面亦同(圖1)，取下背鰭(圖2)，續用刀尖切至腹部取出內臟(圖3)洗淨，將1料煮開，放入魚，蓋上鍋蓋，中火煮約8分鐘後熄火。

■金菇切除頭部老莖，豌豆川燙漂涼切絲，備用。

■油2大匙燒熱，將金菇、紅白蘿蔔絲炒軟，並入¼杯的魚湯，煮開後加豌豆絲拌勻。

■容器內放入魚及炒好的蔬菜，並注入魚湯，食時擠上檸檬汁即可。

SOY SIMMERED GOLDEN THREAD

SERVES 4

1-1/3 lb. (600 g) golden thread fish (red coat; or other white-fleshed fish)

1
- 1 c. *dashi*
- 2/3 c. rice wine
- 2 T. sugar
- 1/2 c. light-colored soy sauce

7 oz. (200 g) *enoki* (golden mushrooms)

6 Chinese peapods

total of 1-1/4 c.: shredded carrot, shredded Chinese white radish

1/4 lemon

■ Cut the fish down to the bone starting from the upper back portion. Turn over the fish and repeat the same cut (illus. 1). Remove the back fins (illus. 2). Continue cutting down to the belly with the tip of the knife. Remove the entrails (illus. 3) and wash the fish. Put 1 in a pot and bring to a boil. Add the fish and cover the pot. Cook over medium heat about 8 minutes, then turn off the heat.

■ Remove the tough ends from the *enoki*. Blanch the peapods in boiling water, then place in a bowl of tap water to cool. Shred and set aside.

■ Heat 2 tablespoons oil in a frying pan and add the *enoki*, and the shredded carrot and white radish. Stir-fry until soft, then add 1/4 cup of liquid from cooking the fish. Bring to a boil, add the shredded peapods, and stir.

■ Place the fish and the stir-fried ingredients on a serving dish. Pour the liquid from cooking the fish over the top. Squeeze on a little lemon juice before eating.

筑前煮

ちくぜんに　　4人份

蒟蒻⋯⋯⋯⋯⋯⋯⋯⋯⋯⋯⋯⋯⅛塊
雞肉(或里肌肉)⋯⋯⋯⋯⋯⋯150公克
筍⋯⋯⋯⋯⋯⋯⋯⋯⋯⋯⋯⋯⋯60公克
紅蘿蔔⋯⋯⋯⋯⋯⋯⋯⋯⋯⋯40公克
牛蒡⋯⋯⋯⋯⋯⋯⋯⋯⋯⋯⋯80公克
香菇⋯⋯⋯⋯⋯⋯⋯⋯⋯⋯⋯⋯4朵
蓮藕⋯⋯⋯⋯⋯⋯⋯⋯⋯⋯⋯60公克

|1| 水⋯⋯⋯⋯⋯⋯⋯⋯⋯⋯⋯3杯 |
| | 醋⋯⋯⋯⋯⋯⋯⋯⋯⋯1大匙 |

煮出汁⋯⋯⋯⋯⋯⋯⋯⋯⋯1½杯

|2| 糖⋯⋯⋯⋯⋯⋯⋯⋯⋯1½大匙 |
| | 味醂⋯⋯⋯⋯⋯⋯⋯⋯1大匙 |

醬油⋯⋯⋯⋯⋯⋯⋯⋯⋯2½大匙
四季豆⋯⋯⋯⋯⋯⋯⋯⋯⋯⋯5條

■蒟蒻切片中央劃一刀(圖1)反轉(圖2)以開水川燙備用。

■雞肉切塊,筍、紅蘿蔔切滾刀塊,牛蒡削片(圖3),香菇泡軟劃十字形,蓮藕切片後順穴修飾出花樣,並與牛蒡同泡1料備用。

■鍋熱加油1大匙,將雞肉及上述各項略炒,倒入煮出汁燒開改小火續煮約15分鐘,再加2料煮至汁將收乾,最後加醬油及四季豆煮至汁收乾即成。

□材料可依個人喜好加以變化,如以白菜、小芋頭、海帶結、木耳青豆仁等代替亦可。

CHIKUZEN NI

SERVES 4

1/3 cake *konnyaku* (devil's tongue paste)
1/3 lb. (150 g) chicken meat (or lean pork)
2 oz. (60 g) bamboo shoots
1-1/3 oz. (40 g) carrot
2-2/3 oz. (80 g) burdock root (*gobō*)
4 dried Chinese black mushrooms (*shiitake*)
2 oz. (60 g) lotus root

|1| 3 c. water |
| | 1 T. rice vinegar |

1-1/2 c. *dashi*

|2| 1-1/2 T. sugar |
| | 1 T. *mirin* (sweet rice wine) |

2-1/2 T. soy sauce
5 string beans

■ Cut the *konnyaku* into slices, and make a slit in the center of each slice (illus. 1). Pull one end through the center (illus. 2). Blanch in boiling water and set aside.

■ Cut the chicken into chunks. Roll-cut the bamboo shoots and carrots. Shave off slices from the burdock root (illus. 3). Soak the dried mushrooms until soft, and make a large crisscross cut in the center of each. Slice the lotus root and cut along the holes to make the slices into an attractive pattern. Marinate the lotus root together with the burdock root in 1 and set aside.

■ Heat a frying pan and add 1 tablespoon oil. Stir-fry the chicken and other above ingredients briefly. Add the *dashi* and bring to a boil. Lower the heat and continue to simmer another 15 minutes or so. Add 2 and cook until the sauce is reduced. Finally, add the soy sauce and string beans, and cook until the sauce is again reduced. Serve.

□ The ingredients used in this recipe may be varied to suit individual taste, for example, Chinese cabbage, taro (dasheen), kelp (*kombu*) strips tied in knots, wood ears, peas, and so forth can be used.

金平牛蒡

ごぼうと牛肉のきんぴら　　　4人份

■選購表皮溼潤有彈性之新鮮牛蒡（圖1），用刀背刮去皮（圖2）洗淨，切4公分長段再切絲（圖3）或直接刨絲，浸1料以免變黑，炒前瀝乾水份。

■鍋熱加麻油，入牛肉絲及牛蒡絲，以大火將水份炒乾，倒入2料繼續炒約3分鐘至汁收乾盛起，並撒上白芝麻即可。

□喜食辣味者，可加紅辣椒絲同炒。

□此道菜放入冰箱冷藏後食用亦別具風味。

牛蒡		180公克
1	水	3杯
	醋	1大匙
麻油		1大匙
嫩牛肉絲		200公克
2	水、醬油	各3大匙
	糖	4大匙
	油	2大匙
白芝麻（炒好）		1大匙

BEEF WITH BURDOCK ROOT

SERVES 4

■ Choose fresh burdock root with a firm, moist skin (illus. 1). Scrape with the dull edge of a knife to peel (illus. 2), and wash. Cut into 1-1/2" (4 cm) sections, then shred with a knife (illus. 3) or a shredder. Soak in 1 to prevent discoloration. Drain well before use.

■ Add the sesame oil to a frying pan, then put in the shredded beef and shredded burdock root. Stir-fry over high heat until dry. Add 2 and continue stir-frying about 3 minutes until the sauce is reduced. Transfer to a serving dish. Sprinkle the toasted white sesame seeds over the top and serve.

□ Those who like spicy-hot food can stir-fry some shredded red chili pepper with the beef and burdock root.

□ This dish can also be refrigerated after cooking and eaten cold.

	6 oz. (180 g) burdock root (*gobō*)
1	3 c. water
	1 T. rice vinegar
	1 T. sesame oil
	7 oz. (200 g) tender beef, shredded
2	3 T. each: water, soy sauce
	4 T. sugar
	2 T. oil.
	1 T. white sesame seeds, toasted

煮昆布小魚

こんぶ巻き煮　　　4人份

乾海帶(60公分)··············	1 條
小魚干·······················75公克
干瓢(泡軟)···················20公克
1	煮出汁······················	2 杯
	醬油·······················3 大匙
	砂糖·······················2 大匙
	酒·························3 大匙

■將全部材料備妥(圖1)，乾海帶用濕布擦乾淨，切與小魚干同長短備用。

■小魚干泡水約5分鐘，去除頭和內臟(圖2)。

■取一段海帶，中央置小魚干(圖3)捲成筒狀，並以干瓢繫緊，放入小鍋，調1料煮至汁將收乾即成。

□喜食辣味者可加紅辣椒同煮。

SIMMERED KOMBU-FISH ROLLS

SERVES 4

1 strip dried kelp seaweed
  (*kombu*; 2' or 60 cm)
2-1/2 oz. (75 g) small dried fish
2/3 oz. (20 g) dried gourd
  shavings (*kampyō*), soaked
  until soft (see p. 69, Basic
  Rolled Sushi)
  2 c. *dashi*
1 3 T. soy sauce
  2 T. sugar
  3 T. rice wine

■ Have all the ingredients ready (illus. 1). Wipe the kelp clean with a damp cloth. Cut into pieces about the same length as the small dried fish. Set aside.

■ Soak the small dried fish in water for about 5 minutes. Remove the heads and entrails (illus. 2).

■ Place some of the small dried fish in the center of each piece of kelp (illus. 3), roll into a cylinder, and tie tightly with a dried gourd shaving. Place in a small saucepan. Mix 1 until blended. Cook the kelp rolls in 1 until the sauce thickens and is almost completely reduced.

□ Red chili pepper may be added when cooking for a spicy-hot flavor.

冬瓜蟹肉

とうがんとかにくず煮　　　4人份

■ 冬瓜去籽，切成4公分四方塊，去皮（圖1），入開水內川燙約1分鐘，撈起備用，香菇泡軟切斜片。

■ 鍋入煮出汁燒開，續入冬瓜以大火煮開，再改小火續煮約20分鐘至冬瓜熟爛透明時，盛入湯碗。

■ 餘汁內加入蟹肉及香菇片煮開，調1料，並以2料勾芡，淋在冬瓜上，擺上薑末即可。

□ 除蟹肉罐頭外，也可用新鮮蟹蒸熟去殼取肉（圖2、3）或以干貝、蝦仁、蛤蜊等代替。

冬瓜………	600公克、香菇………………	3朵
煮出汁………………………………		5杯
蟹肉（罐頭）………………………		1罐
1	塩………………………………	½小匙
	醬油…………………………	½大匙
	味精…………………………	⅛小匙
2	太白粉………………………	3大匙
	水……………………………	2½大匙
薑末…………………………………		1⅓大匙

WINTERMELON WITH CRABMEAT

SERVES 4

■ Remove the seeds from the wintermelon, cut into 1-1/2″ (4 cm) cubes, and peel (illus. 1). Blanch in boiling water about 1 minute, remove, and set aside. Soak the dried mushrooms until soft and cut diagonally into slices.

■ Pour the *dashi* into a pot and bring to a boil. Next add the wintermelon cubes and bring to a second boil over high heat. Turn the heat to low and simmer about 20 minutes, until the wintermelon is cooked through, i.e. soft and translucent. Transfer the wintermelon to a serving bowl.

■ Add the crabmeat and mushroom to the remaining liquid and bring to a boil. Mix in 1, and then 2 to thicken. Pour over the wintermelon, top with the minced ginger root, and serve.

□ Fresh crab may be used instead of canned in this recipe. Steam the crabs until done, and remove the meat (illus. 2, 3). Scallops, shrimp, or clams may also be substituted.

1-1/3 lb. (600 g) wintermelon (wax gourd; *tōgan*)
3 dried Chinese black mushrooms (*shiitake*)
5 c. *dashi*
1 can crabmeat

1 |
1/2′ t. salt
1/2 T. soy sauce
1/8 t. MSG (*ajinomoto*; optional)

2 |
3 T. cornstarch
2-1/2 T. water
1-1/3 T. minced ginger root

本料理由七都里餐廳提供

生烤香魚

鮎の塩焼き　4人份

香魚4條	450公克
鐵串（長40公分）	4支
塩	4大匙
短鐵串（長15公分）	2支
檸檬	½個

■取一尾香魚，頭朝右腹部向內，鐵串由眼部插入（圖1）似魚游水姿勢，使尾部翹起（圖2），在魚鰭及尾部抹上多量的塩作爲裝飾，魚身撒⅛小匙塩，每兩支鐵串合併再串入短鐵串（圖3），以便翻面

■烤箱燒熱約350°F至400°F，將魚置上層烤約5分鐘至表皮略焦肉熟，取出鐵串盛盤，淋上檸檬汁趁熱供食。

■食用時先用筷子將魚壓平，再將魚背朝上輕壓數下，取出頭部及中骨就更方便取食。

□此道菜上桌時魚腹必須面對客人才有禮貌。

□除香魚外，亦可用秋刀魚、鯛魚或其他新鮮魚類來做。

BROILED RIVER TROUT

SERVES 4

4 river trout (ayu) (1 lb. or 450 g)
4 metal skewers (16" or 40 cm long)
4 T. salt
2 short metal skewers (6" or 15 cm long)
1/2 lemon

■ Point the head of the river trout to the right and the belly towards you. Insert a skewer in each, entering at the eye (illus. 1), and making the tail portion stick up, so that the fish looks as though suspended in a swimming posture (illus. 2). Rub salt onto the fin and tail portions of the fish as a garnish. Sprinkle 1/8 teaspoon salt over the body. Skewer the fish together in pairs with the shorter skewers (illus. 3) to facilitate turning the fish over.

■ Preheat the oven to 350° to 400°F (177° to 204°C). Broil the fish on the upper rack of the oven about 5 minutes, until it is cooked through and the skin is golden brown. Remove the skewers and place the fish in a serving dish. Squeeze some lemon juice over the top, and eat while hot.

■ To eat, first flatten the fish by pressing down on it with a pair of chopsticks. Turn the fish so the back is facing upwards, and press down a few times. Removing the head and center bone will make the fish even easier to eat.

□ According to Japanese custom, the belly of fish must face the guest when serving this dish; placing it otherwise would be considered impolite.

□ Mackerel pike, porgy, or other fresh fish may be used in this recipe.

本料理由七都里餐廳 提供

烤鮮鰻片

うなぎの蒲焼き　　4人份

■鰻魚洗淨切去頭尾（圖１）分切４片備用。
■將１料置容器內，放入鰻魚浸30分鐘後取出，餘汁煮開備用。
■將鐵串由鰻魚皮部與肉部之間旋轉串入（圖２）。烤網塗油，將串好的鰻魚置其上（圖３），移入烤箱上層以450°Ｆ 烤，邊烤邊刷上煮好的餘汁（約３～４次），烤約６分鐘至兩面呈金黃略焦時，旋轉取出鐵串，刷少許蜂蜜以增風味，並撒上白芝麻或花椒粉即成。
□如無烤箱，亦可以木炭烤。
□白芝麻炒法參考第43頁芝麻泥拌菠菜做法。

鰻魚１條（長約35公分）	………	淨重450公克
1	砂糖	………………………… 2大匙
	醬油	………………………… 6大匙
	味醂	………………………… 4大匙
	薑汁、酒	………………… 各少許
鐵串（或竹串）	…………………………… 數支
蜂蜜	……………………………… 1 小匙
白芝麻（炒好）	…………………… 1 大匙
或花椒粉	………………………… ⅛小匙

BROILED FRESH EEL (Unagi Kabayaki)

SERVES 4

■ Wash the eel and cut off the head and tail (illus. 1). Cut into 4 equal portions and set aside.
■ Place 1 in a bowl, then add the eel pieces to marinate. Remove after 30 minutes. Put the remaining liquid in a pot, bring to a boil, turn off the heat, and set aside.
■ Insert the skewers just between the skin and flesh of the eel, spiraling the fish around the skewer (illus. 2). Oil a baking rack, and place the skewered eel on top (illus. 3). Place on the upper shelf of the oven and broil at 450°F (232°C). Baste the eel with the leftover marinade as the eel is broiling (about 3 to 4 times). Broil about 6 minutes until both sides are golden brown. Remove the skewers, brush some honey on the eel for extra flavor, and sprinkle with toasted white sesame seeds or ground Szechuan pepper. Serve.
□ If you do not have an oven, the eel can be charcoal grilled.
□ See p. 43, Spinach with Sesame Paste, for instructions on how to toast white sesame seeds.

1 fresh eel (*unagi*; about 14" or 35 cm long, 1 lb. or 450 g net weight)
2 T. sugar
6 T. soy sauce
1　4 T. *mirin* (sweet rice wine)
dash each: ginger root juice, rice wine
8 metal or bamboo skewers
1 t. honey
1 T. white sesame seeds, toasted or 1/8 t. ground Szechuan pepper

烤雞肉串

焼きとり　　4人份

雞腿肉	················	400公克
洋葱(小)	················	1個
或葱	················	3枝
青椒(去籽)	················	2個
1 醬油、味醂	················	各⅓杯
砂糖	················	4大匙
麵粉	················	1大匙
檸檬	················	½個

■雞腿肉、洋葱、青椒分別切2公分四方小塊,取竹串依順序串上洋葱、青椒、雞肉(圖1),至最上端用一片洋葱固定(圖2),檸檬分切四塊。

■煮開1料待涼,將肉串放入浸泡10分鐘取出。

■烤箱燒熱至450°F,肉串置上層烤約4分鐘後,翻面並刷上浸肉汁續烤4分鐘至肉略焦即可。

□亦可用炭火烤(圖3),一面烤,一面刷上浸肉汁至肉熟略焦即可食時可隨個人喜愛撒上花椒粉、胡椒粉、七味辣粉。

BROILED CHICKEN KEBABS (Yakitori)

SERVES 4

14 oz. (400 g) chicken leg meat
1 small onion
  or three green onions
2 green peppers, seeded

1
  1/3 c. each: soy sauce, *mirin*
    (sweet rice wine)
  4 T. sugar
  1 T. flour

1/2 lemon

■ Cut the chicken leg meat, onion, and green peppers into 3/4″ (2 cm) cubes. On bamboo skewers, skewer the onion, green pepper, and chicken cubes (illus. 1) alternately until the skewer is full. Top with a piece of onion to secure the kebab (illus. 2). Quarter the lemon.

■ Bring 1 to a boil, then allow to cool. Marinate the kebabs in the sauce for 10 minutes. Remove.

■ Heat the oven to 450°F (232°C) and broil the kebabs on the top shelf for 4 minutes. Turn over and brush on some of the leftover marinade. Broil another 4 minutes, until the meat is golden brown. Serve.

□ The kebabs can also be charcoal-grilled (illus. 3). Brush on the marinade as the kebabs are grilling. Grill until the chicken is cooked through and golden brown. Before eating, ground Szechuan pepper, ground black pepper, or seven-flavor seasoning (*shichimi-tōgarashi*) may be sprinkled over the kebabs, according to individual preference.

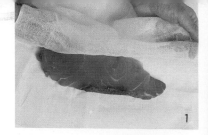

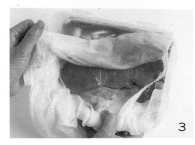

本料理由七都里餐廳 提供

味噌烤魚

魚の味噌焼き　　　4人份

■魚肉洗淨，加塩醃約30分鐘。

■將魚的塩份洗淨，再以酒1大匙淋洗一次，拭乾，以白紗布包好祇能包一層（圖1），置調好的1料內（圖2），浸泡約1天，將紗布攤開，取出魚片（圖3）洗淨，烤箱燒熱約350°F 至 400°F，以中火烤熟（約5分鐘），食時淋上檸檬汁。

□亦可選用其他刺少的魚類，如鰰魚、鱈魚、鮠魚等代替。

□味噌漬魚肉可漬2至3天，但不宜超過3天，否則魚的鮮味會流失在味噌中，漬蔬菜亦同。

鱵魚2片		300公克
塩		⅛小匙
白紗布		1塊
1	白味噌	400公克
	味酥	3大匙
	酒、糖	各2大匙
檸檬		½個

BROILED FISH PICKLED IN MISO (Misoyaki)

SERVES 4

■ Wash the fish. Cure in salt for 30 minutes.

■ Wash the salt off the fish, then sprinkle 1 tablespoon rice wine over the fish, and dry. Wrap in one layer of white cheesecloth (illus. 1). Mix 1 thoroughly and allow the fish to pickle in it (illus. 2) for about one day. Open the cheesecloth and remove the fish steaks (illus. 3). Rinse clean. Broil in the oven under medium heat (350° to 400°F or 177° to 204°C) until done, about five minutes. Squeeze on some lemon juice before serving.

□ Other types of fish that do not have too many bones may be used in this recipe, such as oil fish, cod, or slate cod croaker, etc.

□ The fish may be pickled in the miso for 2 to 3 days, but no more than 3 days; otherwise the fresh flavor of the fish will be absorbed into the miso paste. The same is true when pickling vegetables.

2 marlin (kajiki) steaks (2/3 lb. or 300 g)	
1/8 t. salt	
1 square cheesecloth	
1	14 oz. (400 g) white miso
	3 T. mirin (sweet rice wine)
	2 T. each: rice wine, sugar
1/2 lemon	

煎卷蛋

出し巻き卵　　4人份

蛋		6個
1	煮出汁	5 大匙
	塩	1/2 小匙
	淡口醬油	2/3 小匙
	砂糖	2/3 小匙

■盆內置蛋6個打散，調入1料輕輕打勻(不宜打起泡沫)。
■平底鍋燒熱，用棉花(或紗布)沾油，輕輕擦上一層，將蛋汁倒入約3大匙，以小火煎薄薄的一層蛋皮，用筷子捲起成蛋卷狀(圖1)推至一邊，再塗上一層油續倒入3大匙蛋汁煎成薄蛋皮，將煎好蛋卷連同第二張蛋皮一併捲上，再推至一邊(圖2)，依此要領，將蛋汁全部煎完，蛋皮一層層反覆捲上，做完時厚度約有3公分，反扣竹簾上(圖3)並捲緊，待涼切塊盛盤即可。
□蛋汁內亦可加入烤好的鰻魚絲及各種熟材料以增風味。

JAPANESE EGG ROLL

SERVES 4

1	6 eggs
	5 T. *dashi*
	1/2 t. salt
	2/3 t. light-colored soy sauce
	2/3 t. sugar

■ Crack the 6 eggs into a bowl and beat lightly. Gently mix in 1 until well blended (do not beat until foamy).

■ Heat a flat-bottomed frying pan. Lightly oil the bottom, using a wad of cotton or cheesecloth. Pour about 3 tablespoons of the egg mixture into the pan. Fry into a thin layer of egg over low heat. Roll up the egg "pancake" with a pair of chopsticks (illus. 1). Place near the edge of the pan. Oil the bottom of the pan again, add 3 tablespoons of the egg mixture, and fry into another thin egg pancake. The second egg pancake will be attached to the first; wrap the second around the first. Again place it near the edge of the pan (illus.2). Repeat this process until the egg mixture is used up. When complete, the egg roll should stand about 1-1/2" (3cm) high. Place on a bamboo *sushi* mat (*sudare*; illus. 3), and roll tightly. Allow to cool, cut, and arrange in a serving dish. Serve.

□ Cooked shredded eel or other cooked foods may be added to the egg mixture for variety.

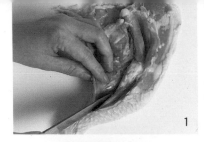

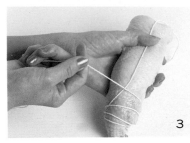

煎鷄肉捲

鶏肉の包み焼き　　　4人份

■雞腿由中間劃開一刀，去骨（圖1）片成厚薄均勻的大薄片（圖2），
加塩½小匙、酒1小匙醃15分鐘，小黃瓜分切4等份長條並去籽，
1料煮熟切丁備用。

■鍋入1料及2料煮2分鐘使其入味，蛋打散加入拌炒（須不斷攪
拌至蛋凝固）待涼即為餡。

■將雞肉片攤開，上撒麵粉，放上½的餡和小黃瓜捲成筒狀，以棉
繩紮緊（圖3），餘½做法亦同。

■平底鍋燒熱，加油1大匙，大火將肉捲煎呈金黃色，移入蒸籠蒸
15分鐘，取出置鍋，調3料續煮至汁收乾，待涼取下棉繩，切圓片
排盤即成。

	雞腿2隻	約600公克
	小黃瓜	1條
1	紅蘿蔔、筍	各40公克
	香菇（泡軟）	1朵
2	煮出汁……¼杯、砂糖	2大匙
	塩……⅛小匙、淡口醬油	1小匙
	蛋……3個、麵粉	2小匙
	棉繩（60公分）	2條
3	醬油、砂糖、味醂	各3大匙
	麵粉	½小匙

STUFFED CHICKEN ROLLS

SERVES 4

■ Cut down the middle of each chicken leg, and remove the bone
(illus. 1). Carefully cut the chicken with linked slices so that a large
sheet of chicken of even thickness results (illus. 2). Marinate in 1/2
teaspoon salt and 1 teaspoon rice wine for 15 minutes. Quarter
the gherkin cucumbers lengthwise and scrape out the seeds. Cook
1 until soft, cube, and set aside.

■ Add 1 and 2 to a pot and cook 2 minutes, so that the flavors
are well absorbed. Beat the eggs lightly and add to the pot. Stir
constantly until the egg becomes firm. Allow to cool. This is the
filling.

■ Spread open the chicken and sprinkle on some flour. Add 1/2
of the filling and some gherkin cucumber. Roll into a cylindrical
shape. Secure with a string (illus. 3). Repeat for the second piece
of chicken.

■ Heat a frying pan and add 1 tablespoon oil. Fry the chicken
rolls over high heat until golden brown, then transfer to a steamer.
Steam 15 minutes. Remove and place in a pot. Mix 3 and add
to the pot. Cook until the sauce is reduced. Allow the chicken rolls
to cool, then remove the strings. Slice into rounds and arrange on
a plate. Serve.

	2 chicken legs (about 1-1/3 lb. or 600 g)
	1 gherkin cucumber
1	1-1/3 oz. (40 g) each: carrot, bamboo shoots
	1 dried Chinese black mushroom (*shiitake*; soaked until soft)
2	1/4 c. *dashi*
	2 T. sugar
	1/8 t. salt
	1 t. light-colored soy sauce
	3 eggs
	2 t. flour
	2 lengths of string, 2' (60 cm) each
3	3 T. each: soy sauce, sugar, *mirin*
	1/2 t. flour

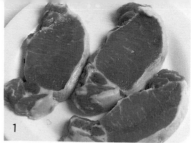

薑煎猪排

豚肉の生姜焼き　　　4人份

里肌肉	300公克
1　醬油	3大匙
味酥	2大匙
糖、酒	各1大匙
薑片	12片
四季豆	8條

■里肌肉切片(圖1)並用刀背拍鬆(圖2)白筋處劃2～3刀(圖3)以免煎時緊縮，置調勻的1料內醃約30分鐘，四季豆川燙切段。

■平底鍋燒熱，加油1大匙，將肉片放入煎至兩面呈金黃色後鏟出盛盤。

■將浸肉汁倒回鍋內，中火燒煮至汁剩一半呈濃稠狀時，取出薑片置盤邊，餘汁淋在肉片上，旁置四季豆即成。

PORK CUTLETS WITH GINGER

SERVES 4

2/3 lb. (300 g) lean pork
1
3 T. soy sauce
2 T. *mirin* (sweet rice wine)
1 T. each: sugar, rice wine
12 slices ginger root
8 string beans

■ Slice the pork (illus. 1) and tenderize with the dull edge of a cleaver (illus. 2). Make 2 to 3 slashes into the white sinew areas (illus. 3) to prevent shrinking while frying. Blend 1 and marinate the pork in it for about 30 minutes. Blanch the string beans in boiling water and cut into pieces.

■ Heat a flat-bottomed frying pan, add 1 tablespoon oil, and place the pork in the pan. Fry on both sides until golden. Remove from pan and arrange on a serving plate.

■ Pour the remaining marinade liquid into the frying pan and cook over medium heat until it is reduced to about half of its original volume and is thick. Garnish with the ginger root slices, then pour the cooked marinade over the pork. Garnish with the string beans and serve.

本料理由七都里餐廳 提供

本料理由七都里餐廳 提供

生烤墨魚

いかの照焼　　4人份

■ 墨魚去頭及內臟，並剝除身上的皮膜，由內側切直刀或花刀（圖1），醃1料約10分鐘。

■ 烤法：備烤網置爐上燒熱，刷上一層油（圖2），將墨魚置其上（圖3），或備烤箱燒熱450°F至500°F，將墨魚置烤盤，放入烤箱上層以大火烤，邊烤邊刷上2料，烤至兩面焦紅即可盛盤，食時淋上檸檬汁。

■ 煎法：平底鍋燒熱，加油2大匙，放入墨魚煎至兩面呈金黃色，再淋上2料，煎至汁收乾即可盛盤，食時淋上檸檬汁。

□ 亦可以紅薑、罐裝白果裝飾搭配食用，看來更可口，入口更有味。

□ 可灑上黑芝麻或刷上雲丹醬同烤。

	墨魚1條	約300公克
1	塩	½小匙
	酒、味酥	各1大匙
2	味酥	1大匙
	糖	1大匙
	檸檬片	4片

BROILED SQUID

SERVES 4

■ Remove the head, entrails, and outer membrane from the squid. Score the inside with parallel or cross cuts (illus. 1). Marinate in 1 about 10 minutes.

■ Broiling method: Heat a baking rack on top of a charcoal grill, oil (illus. 2), and place the squid on the rack (illus. 3). Or, heat the oven to 450° to 550°F (232° to 260°C), place the squid in a baking dish, and broil at high heat on the top shelf. Brush on 2 frequently while it is broiling. Broil until both sides have a deep caramel color. Place on a serving plate. Squeeze some lemon juice over the top before eating.

■ Pan-frying method: Heat a flat-bottomed frying pan and add 2 tablespoons oil. Add the squid and fry until both sides are golden brown. Sprinkle on 2. Fry until the sauce is almost completely reduced. Transfer to a serving plate. Squeeze some lemon juice over the top before eating.

□ The serving plate may be garnished with pickled red ginger root (beni-shōga) and canned gingko nuts for added taste variety and visual appeal.

□ Black sesame seeds may be sprinkled on, or uni paste may be brushed on the squid while broiling.

1 squid (ika; about 2/3 lb. or 300 g)

1
1/2 t. salt
1 T. each: rice wine, mirin

2
1 T. mirin
1 T. sugar
4 slices lemon

鋁紙鷄肉

鶏肉の銀紙焼き　　　4人份

雞肉	………………………	450公克
新鮮香菇(大)	…………………	1朵
青椒	………………………	½個
洋蔥(小)	…… 1個、紅辣椒	………2條

1	味酥、醬油	……………各3大匙
	酒	……………………2大匙

鋁箔紙(20公分×20公分)	…………	4張
玻璃紙(20公分×20公分)	…………	4張
奶油(或沙拉油)	……………………	2小匙
檸檬	……………………………	½個

■雞肉切8塊(約3公分×2公分)，香菇、青椒、洋蔥、紅辣椒分別切絲，並調1料浸泡約10分鐘。

■鋁箔紙上舖玻璃紙，再塗上奶油(圖1)備用。

■將浸好各料分成四等份，取一份放在已塗油之玻璃紙上(圖2)，對摺由兩端包起(圖3)。

■烤箱燒熱至450°F，將包好的雞肉置烤箱中層烤約15分鐘，取出置盤，食時淋入檸檬汁即可。

CHICKEN IN FOIL

SERVES 4

1 lb. (450 g) chicken meat
1 large fresh Chinese black
　mushroom (*shiitake*)
1/2 green pepper
1 small onion
2 small red chili peppers

1 | 3 T. each: *mirin*, soy sauce
　2 T. rice wine

4 sheets aluminum foil, 8″ (20
　cm) square
4 sheets cellophane, 8″ (20
　cm) square
2 t. butter (or cooking oil)
1/2 lemon

■ Cut the chicken into 8 pieces (about 1-1/4″×3/4″ or 3×2 cm). Cut the mushroom, green pepper, onion, and red chili peppers into julienne strips. Marinate in 1 about 10 minutes.

■ Place a sheet of cellophane on top of each sheet of aluminum foil. Grease each sheet of cellophane with the butter or oil (illus. 1). Set aside.

■ Divide the combined marinated ingredients into 4 equal portions. Place one portion on each of the buttered cellophane sheets (illus. 2). Fold in half, then wrap into a package (illus. 3).

■ Heat the oven to 450°F (232°C). Bake the chicken packets on the middle shelf for about 15 minutes. Remove and place on a serving plate. Open and squeeze some lemon juice over the top to eat.

茶壺蒸海鮮

土瓶蒸し　　　4人份

■雞肉、魚肉洗淨切片，檸檬分切4片，貝芽菜（圖1）切段，蛤蜊、鮮香菇洗淨備妥（圖2）。

■將雞肉醃⅛小匙塩與魚肉、蛤蜊分別以開水川燙撈出。

■茶壺內放入雞肉、魚肉、蛤蜊、香菇及煮開的1料，蓋上蓋子移入蒸籠，大火蒸3分鐘取出，撒上貝芽菜並立即蓋好，即可趁熱食用。食時淋上檸檬汁，先倒汁品嚐（圖3），再吃壺內材料。

□材料亦可選用金菇、鮑魚菇、豬肉、蝦、魚板等。

□如無茶壺，可用盅或碗代替。

雞肉	··········	40公克
魚肉	··········	40公克
檸檬（小）	··········	½個
貝芽菜（蘿蔔嬰）	··········	適量
蛤蜊	··········	40公克
鮮香菇（小）	··········	4朵
1	煮出汁	3杯
	塩	⅔小匙
	淡口醬油	少許

SEAFOOD IN A TEAPOT

SERVES 4

■ Wash and slice the chicken and fish. Cut the lemon into 4 slices. Cut the white radish sprouts (illus. 1) into sections. Wash the clams and mushrooms and set aside (illus. 2).

■ Marinate the chicken in 1/8 teaspoon salt. Blanch the chicken, fish, and clams separately in boiling water.

■ Bring 1 to a boil. Add the chicken, fish, clams, mushrooms, and 1 to a teapot. Cover and place in a steamer. Steam over high heat for 3 minutes, then remove. Sprinkle the white radish sprouts over the top and replace the cover immediately. Serve hot. Squeeze some lemon juice over the top, then pour out some of the liquid to taste (illus. 3) before eating.

□ Other ingredients may be used in this recipe, such as enoki, abalone mushrooms, pork, shrimp, fish cake, and so forth.

□ If a teapot is unavailable, a bowl or casserole dish may be substituted.

1-1/3 oz. (40 g) chicken meat
1-1/3 oz. (40 g) fish fillet
1/2 small lemon
white radish sprouts (*kaiware*), as desired
1-1/3 oz. (40 g) clams
4 small fresh Chinese black mushrooms (*shiitake*)

1	3 c. *dashi*
	2/3 t. salt
	dash of light-colored soy sauce

茶碗蒸

茶わん蒸し　　4人份

雞腿肉	60公克
1 ｜醬油、糖	各⅛小匙
鮮蝦4條	75公克
鮮香菇(小) 4朶、蛋	4個
2 ｜煮出汁 3杯、塩	1½小匙
｜淡口醬油、味醂	各1小匙
魚板(切花刀)	4片
菠菜(燙熟切段)	1棵
檸檬皮	適量

■雞肉切8小塊，醃1料，鮮蝦去背殼留頭尾殼，鮮香菇切十字形(圖1)蛋打散置容器內，倒入2料拌勻過濾備用。

■將材料分四等份，取一份放入蒸碗(依序放雞肉、蝦、魚板、香菇)，並注入蛋汁約八分滿，取出泡沫(圖2)，移入蒸籠，水開大火蒸1～2分鐘後改小火續蒸約15分鐘(火候的控制極爲重要)，擺上菠菜及檸檬皮，蓋上碗蓋即成。

□亦可用電鍋(外鍋水2杯)，水開蒸約10分鐘，以竹籤插入不流出蛋汁即可，但必須在蒸碗上蓋保鮮膜(圖3)或鍋蓋內面鋪上一層白布，以免蒸氣滴入。

SAVORY CUP CUSTARD (Chawan Mushi)

SERVES 4

- 2 oz. (60 g) chicken leg meat
- 1 ⎰ 1/8 t. soy sauce
  ⎱ 1/8 t. sugar
- 4 fresh shrimp (2-1/2 oz. or 75 g)
- 4 small fresh Chinese black mushrooms (shiitake)
- 4 eggs
- 2 ⎰ 3 c. dashi
  ⎪ 1-1/2 t. salt
  ⎱ 1 t. each: light-colored soy sauce, mirin
- 4 slices fish cake (kamaboko; ripple-cut)
- 1 bunch spinach, blanched in boiling water and cut into sections
- lemon peel, as desired

■ Cut the chicken into 8 small pieces and marinate in 1. Remove the shell from the back portion of the shrimp, but leave head and tail intact. Make a crosscut in the center of the mushrooms (illus. 1).

■ Beat the egg lightly and place in a bowl. Mix in 2 and strain.

■ Divide the ingredients up equally four ways. Place one of the portions in each of 4 steaming bowls (follow this order: chicken, shrimp, fish cake, mushroom). Fill each bowl 4/5 full with the egg mixture. Skim off any foam (illus. 2). Place the bowls in a steamer. After bringing the water to a full boil, steam 1 to 2 minutes over high heat. Turn the heat to low and steam for about 15 minutes. It is important to control the heat source carefully when steaming egg. Remove from steamer, place some spinach and lemon peel on top of each, and cover each bowl. Serve.

□ An electric rice cooker can also be used to make this dish. Add 2 cups water to the outer pot and steam about 10 minutes after the water has begun to boil. Test for doneness by inserting a toothpick or bamboo skewer. If no egg flows out as liquid, it is done. You must either cover the bowls with plastic wrap (illus. 3), or place a white towel or cloth inside the rice cooker cover to prevent the condensed steam from dripping into the egg.

蛋豆腐

玉子豆腐　　　4人份

■蛋打散加入調勻的１料拌勻過濾（圖１）。
■將蛋汁倒入模型（圖２、３）或便當盒，並去除表面的泡沫，移入蒸籠以大火蒸１～２分鐘後改小火續蒸15分鐘。
■蒸好蛋豆腐取出待涼，切成４塊置容器，淋上煮好的２料即可食用。
□亦可用電鍋蒸，請參考第39頁茶碗蒸。

雞蛋		4個
1	煮出汁	1½杯
	淡口醬油	¾小匙
	塩、味醂	各¾小匙
2	煮出汁	¾杯
	味醂	1⅔大匙
	淡口醬油	1⅔大匙

MOCK TOFU

SERVES 4

■ Beat the eggs lightly. Mix 1 thoroughly and add to the egg, blending well. Strain (illus. 1).
■ Pour the egg mixture into a small baking pan (illus. 2, 3) or into an Oriental style metal lunchbox (*bento*). Skim off any surface foam. Place in a steamer and steam over high heat 1 to 2 minutes. Turn the heat to low and steam for another 15 minutes.
■ Remove the mock *tofu* and allow to cool. Cut into 4 squares and place on a serving dish. Bring 2 to a boil, then pour over the mock *tofu*. Serve.
□ An electric rice cooker may also be used to make this dish. See p. 39, Savory Cup Custard, for instructions.

4 eggs	
1	1-1/2 c. *dashi*
	3/4 t. light-colored soy sauce
	3/4 t. each: salt, *mirin*
2	3/4 c. *dashi*
	1-2/3 T. *mirin*
	1-2/3 T. light-colored soy sauce

蒸蓮藕泥

はす蒸し　　4人份

蓮藕2節				約300公克
1	醋	1大匙、水		3杯
2	煮出汁	⅓杯、淡口醬油		1小匙
	塩	½小匙、味醂		1小匙
雞腿肉				60公克
3	醬油	⅛小匙、糖		⅛小匙
蝦仁4隻	75公克或白菓			8粒
鮮香菇(小)				4朵
魚板		4片、檸檬皮		少許

■蓮藕(圖1)去皮，浸1料約15分鐘(以免變黑並去澀味)磨成泥(圖2)置盆加入2料拌勻(圖3)備用。

■雞肉切8小塊，拌上3料醃10分鐘。

■蒸碗內放入雞肉、蝦仁、香菇、魚板並倒入蓮藕泥約七分滿，移入蒸籠以小火蒸約30分鐘取出，上撒少許檸檬皮趁熱食用。

□蓮藕以接近頭部的較老，較好吃，帶土的蓮藕可存放一週左右，洗淨的最好當天使用，以保持鮮度。

□亦可以白菓代替蝦仁，乾白菓須先加水蒸30分鐘至熟才可使用，罐裝白菓則可直接使用。

STEAMED LOTUS ROOT PASTE

SERVES 4

	2 links fresh lotus root (*renkon*), about 2/3 lb. (300 g)
1	1 T. rice vinegar
	3 c. water
2	1/2 c. *dashi*
	1 t. light-colored soy sauce
	1/2 t. salt
	1 t. *mirin* (sweet rice wine)
	2 oz. (60 g) chicken leg meat
3	1/8 t. soy sauce
	1/8 t. sugar
	4 shelled shrimp (2-1/2 oz. or 75 g) or 8 gingko nuts
	4 small fresh Chinese black mushrooms (*shiitake*)
	4 slices fish cake (*kamaboko*)
	lemon peel, as desired

■ Peel the lotus root (illus. 1) and soak in 1 about 15 minutes (to prevent discoloration and to remove any raw taste). Grind into a paste (illus. 2) and place in a bowl. Mix in 2 until well blended (illus. 3). Set aside.

■ Cut the chicken into 8 small pieces. Mix in 3 and allow to marinate 10 minutes.

■ Place the chicken, shrimp, mushrooms and fish cake in a steaming bowl, then pour enough of the lotus root paste over the top to fill the bowl about 7/10 full. Place in a steamer and steam 30 minutes over low heat. Remove from steamer and sprinkle a little lemon peel over the top. Serve hot.

□ The portion of the lotus root closest to the top is tougher but tastier. If covered with mud, lotus root can be kept about one week. Once lotus root is washed it is best to use it the same day for maximum freshness.

□ Gingko nuts can be substituted for the shrimp. If using dried gingko nuts, add water and steam 30 minutes before use. Canned gingko nuts may be used as is.

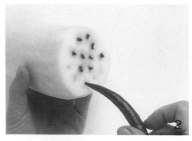

本料理由七都里餐廳提供

鮮魚蒸豆腐

鯛のちり蒸し　　　4人份

■魚肉切4大塊，撒上¼小匙塩備用。

■嫩豆腐每塊切四等份，香菇切星形，乾海帶用濕布擦乾淨，菠菜、紅蘿蔔分別洗淨燙熟切段。

■白蘿蔔用筷子插洞（圖1），再插入去籽的紅辣椒（圖2）磨成泥狀（圖3），加葱花並調1料拌勻，即爲醋汁。

■乾海帶舖容器，上置魚肉、豆腐、香菇、菠菜、紅蘿蔔，加酒2大匙以大火蒸約7～8分鐘取出，擺上嫩薑絲即可趁熱沾醋汁食用。

□亦可選魚刺較少者如鱈魚、鮸魚、加納魚、石斑魚或蝦、蛤蜊、貝類等使用。

鯛魚肉（帶皮）	200公克
嫩豆腐	2塊、香菇（泡軟） 4朵
乾海帶（5～6公分四方片）	4片
菠菜	1棵、紅蘿蔔 4片
白蘿蔔	75公克、紅辣椒 1條
葱花（綠色部份）	4大匙
1　醬油	4大匙
醋、檸檬汁	各1⅔大匙
嫩薑絲	少許

FRESH FISH STEAMED WITH TOFU

SERVES 4

■ Cut the porgy fillets into 4 large pieces. Sprinkle on 1/4 teaspoon salt and set aside.

■ Cut each cake of *tofu* into 4 equal pieces. Score the mushrooms with three intersecting cuts to form a star in the center. Wipe the kelp clean with a damp cloth. Wash the spinach and carrot, blanch each separately in boiling water, and cut into sections.

■ Insert a chopstick several times into the white radish to make a number of "wells" (illus.1). Stuff the red chili pepper strips inside (illus.2). Grind into a puree (illus.3). Add the chopped green onion. Mix in 1 thoroughly. This is the vinegar dip.

■ Spread open the kelp in a bowl. Place the fish, *tofu*, mushrooms, spinach, and carrot on top. Sprinkle on 2 tablespoons rice wine. Steam over high heat about 7 to 8 minutes. Remove. Top with shredded young ginger root. Serve hot, with the vinegar dip on the side.

□ Other fish (that does not have too many bones) may be used in this recipe, such as cod, slate cod croaker, Spanish mackerel (*sawara*), or grouper; or shrimp, clams, other shellfish, and so forth.

7 oz. (200 g) porgy fillet (red sea bream; skin on)
2 cakes soft *tofu*
4 dried Chinese black mushrooms (soaked until soft)
4 pieces dried kelp seaweed (*kombu*), 2 to 2-1/2" (5 to 6 cm) square
1 bunch spinach
4 slices carrot
2-1/2 oz. (75 g) Chinese white radish (*daikon*)
1 small red chili pepper (seeded and julienned)
4 T. chopped green onion (green portion only)

1　4 T. soy sauce
1-2/3 T. each: rice vinegar, lemon juice
shredded young ginger root, as desired

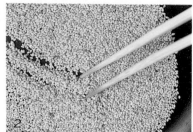

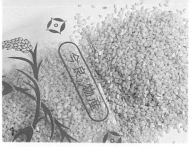

芝麻泥拌菠菜

ほれん草の胡麻お浸し　　　4人份

白芝麻	⋯⋯⋯⋯⋯⋯⋯⋯⋯⋯⋯	2大匙
	糖⋯⋯⋯⋯⋯⋯⋯⋯⋯⋯⋯	2小匙
1	醬油⋯⋯⋯⋯⋯⋯⋯⋯⋯⋯	2大匙
	煮出汁⋯⋯⋯⋯⋯⋯⋯⋯⋯	2小匙
菠菜	⋯⋯⋯⋯⋯⋯⋯⋯⋯⋯⋯	450公克
柴魚片	⋯⋯⋯⋯⋯⋯⋯⋯⋯⋯	少許

■白芝麻（圖1）洗淨瀝乾，入乾鍋以小火炒香（圖2）碾成粉（圖3）與1料調勻，即成芝麻泥。

■菠菜洗淨，入鍋燙熟約1分鐘，取出漂涼，擠乾水份，切5公分長段置盤，食用時拌入芝麻泥，撒上柴魚片即可。

□除菠菜外，亦可用四季豆、茼蒿菜、小白菜等代替。

□白芝麻亦可先炒熟後直接撒在菠菜上拌食。

SPINACH WITH SESAME PASTE

SERVES 4

	2 T. white sesame seeds
	2 t. sugar
1	2 T. soy sauce
	2 t. *dashi*
	1 lb. (450 g) fresh spinach
	bonito shavings, as desired

■ Wash and drain the white sesame seeds (illus. 1). Toast by heating in a dry frying pan over low heat (use no oil; illus. 2). Grind into a powder (illus. 3) and mix together well with 1. This is the sesame paste.

■ Wash the spinach thoroughly and blanch in boiling water about 1 minute. Rinse in tap water to cool. Squeeze out the excess moisture. Cut into 2" (5 cm) sections. Place in a serving dish. Toss with the sesame paste and top with bonito shavings to serve.

□ Other vegetables, such as string beans, garland chrysanthemum (*shungiku*), Chinese cabbage, and so forth, may be substituted for the spinach.

□ The white sesame seeds may, as an alternative, be toasted and sprinkled directly on the spinach instead of first ground into a powder.

黃醬拌秋葵

オクラの黄身酢和え　　　4人份

■草蝦煮熟去殼備用。
■黃秋葵選細小較嫩者(圖1)加塩⅛小匙輕揉(圖2)洗淨，放入開水川燙漂涼切薄片。
■蛋取蛋黃，放入大湯匙內隔水煮約1分鐘，邊煮邊攪拌，使呈濃稠狀，置碗拌入1料即為黃醬。
■將蝦、黃秋葵置容器，淋入少許黃醬即成。
□食時可撒上柴魚絲(圖3)以增香味。
□如無黃秋葵，可用小黃瓜取代。

草蝦8條	300公克
黃秋葵	4條
蛋	1個

	白醋	1 小匙
1	味酥	⅛小匙
	糖	⅛小匙

OKRA WITH EGG DRESSING

SERVES 4

■ Boil the shrimp until just cooked, shell, and set aside.
■ Small, thin okra is more tender and tastier (illus. 1). Rub gently with 1/8 teaspoon salt (illus. 2). Rinse clean. Blanch in boiling water, cool in tap water, and cut into thin slices.
■ Separate the egg. Transfer the yolk to a large serving spoon, then place the spoon on the surface of boiling water. Stir the yolk carefully with a pair of chopsticks until of a thick consistency, about one minute (it will be about 3/10 cooked). Be extremely careful not to burn yourself on the steam! Place the egg in a bowl and mix in 1, blending thoroughly. This is the egg dressing.
■ Arrange the shrimp and okra on a serving plate. Pour on a small amount of egg dressing and serve.
□ Bonito shavings (illus. 3) may be sprinkled over the top just before eating for extra flavor.
□ If okra is unavailable, gherkin cucumbers may be substituted.

8 shrimp (2/3 lb. or 300 g)
4 okra (ladies' fingers, gumbo)
1 egg

1　1 t. rice vinegar
　　1/8 t. *mirin*
　　1/8 t. sugar

本料理由七都里餐廳提供

酸醋鱆魚

たこ酢　　　4人份

鱆魚	200公克、小黃瓜		2條
海帶芽	75公克、蓮藕		40公克
白醋			2大匙
1	白醋、水		各¼杯
	淡口醬油	1大匙、砂糖	3大匙
	塩	½小匙、柴魚片	10公克
薑泥			適量

■鱆魚(圖1)洗淨,水開入鍋煮約5～6分鐘撈出,待涼切0.3公分斜片。

■小黃瓜洗淨,放入開水川燙3秒鐘後漂冷水(使顏色更翠綠),瀝乾水份,斜45度切花刀,深至½處(圖2),翻面切法相同,刀紋需相連(圖3),切約4公分長段。

■海帶芽將塩份洗淨,擠乾水份,蓮藕順紋切粗條,分別川燙漂涼與切好的小黃瓜同浸白醋。

■煮開1料並過濾,即爲醋汁。

■將鱆魚、黃瓜、海帶芽、蓮藕、薑泥整齊排盤,淋上醋汁即成。

□除鱆魚外,亦可用花枝、蝦來代替。

OCTOPUS SALAD

SERVES 4

7 oz. (200 g) fresh octopus (*tako*)
2 gherkin cucumbers
2-1/2 oz. (75 g) *wakame* (lobe-leaf seaweed)
1-1/3 oz. (40 g) lotus root (*renkon*)
2 T. rice wine

1   1/4 c. each: rice wine, water
    1 T. light-colored soy sauce
    3 T. sugar
    1/2 t. salt
    1/3 oz. (10 g) bonito shavings (*katsuobushi*)
ginger root puree, as desired

■ Wash the octopus (illus. 1). Cook in boiling water about 5 to 6 minutes. Remove, allow to cool, and cut into 1/4" (.3 cm) diagonal slices.

■ Wash the gherkin cucumbers. Blanch in boiling water 3 seconds, then immerse in cold water (this gives the cucumbers a brilliant green color). Drain. Make diagonal (at a 45° angle) crosscuts in the gherkin cucumbers, cutting about halfway through (illus. 2). Turn over the cucumber and cut again in the same way. The cucumber must remain connected (illus. 3). Cut into approximately 2-1/2" (4 cm) pieces.

■ Rinse the *wakame* to remove the salt it contains, then squeeze out the excess moisture. Cut the lotus root into thick strips, following the grain. Blanch the *wakame* and the lotus root separately in boiling water. Marinate in the vinegar, together with the gherkin cucumbers.

■ Bring 1 to a boil and strain. This is the vinegar dressing.

■ Arrange the octopus, cucumber, *wakame*, lotus root, and ginger root puree neatly on a serving plate. Pour the vinegar dressing over the top and serve.

□ Squid or shrimp may be substituted for the octopus in this recipe.

黃瓜捲大蝦

えびのきゅうり巻き　　　4人份

■小黃瓜置板上撒⅛小匙塩揉軟（圖1）洗淨，切0.1公分圓薄片，再加⅛小匙塩醃約5分鐘，擠乾水份浸1料。

■草蝦串上竹串（圖2），入開水燙熟約1分半鐘撈起，以冷開水漂涼，去頭除殼備用。

■竹簾上鋪保鮮膜，將小黃瓜輕輕擠乾，整齊的平鋪於保鮮膜上（儘量不重疊），寬約4公分（圖3），蝦擺中央，捲成長條狀並壓緊，即可將蝦捲置冰箱。

■食前分切12塊，切時刀要利，一刀切下，就不易散開。將保鮮膜輕輕拿掉，整齊排盤，淋上2料即可。

小黃瓜（直）	·······················	2條
1	糖 ·······················	1大匙
	醋 ·······················	½大匙
草蝦4條 ·····················		150公克
竹串 ·······················		4支
竹簾 ·······················		1付
保鮮膜（15公分×15公分）	·········	1張
2	糖 ·······················	2大匙
	醋 ·······················	2大匙

SHRIMP-CUCUMBER ROLLS

SERVES 4

■ Place the cucumbers on a cutting board. Sprinkle 1/8 teaspoon salt over them and gently rub it in to make the cucumbers soft and pliable (illus. 1). Rinse clean. Cut into 1/16″ (.1 cm) thin rounds. Cure in another 1/8 teaspoon salt for 5 minutes. Squeeze out the excess moisture and marinate in 1.

■ Impale one shrimp on each bamboo skewer (illus. 2). Blanch about 1-1/2 minutes in boiling water. Place the shrimp in a bowl of cold water to cool. Pull out the skewers. Remove the heads, shell, and set aside.

■ Place the sheet of plastic wrap on the bamboo mat. Gently squeeze the cucumbers dry and neatly arrange them in a flat, even layer on the plastic wrap, about 1-1/2″ (4 cm) wide (illus. 3); avoid stacking the cucumbers on top of each other. Place the shrimp in the center. Gently roll into a tight cylinder. Place in the refrigerator.

■ Before serving, use a sharp knife to slice the roll into 12 small pieces, cutting with one single downward stroke. Gently remove the plastic wrap. Arrange neatly on a serving dish. Sprinkle 2 over the top and serve.

	2 (straight) gherkin cucumbers
1	1 T. sugar
	1/2 T. rice vinegar
	4 shrimp (1/3 lb. or 150 g)
	bamboo skewers
	bamboo *sushi* mat (*sudare*)
	1 sheet plastic wrap (6″ or 15 cm square)
2	2 T. sugar
	2 T. rice vinegar

雲丹拌蒟蒻

こんにゃくのうに和え　　　4人份

蒟蒻絲	……………………………	225公克
1	塩	⅛小匙
	酒、味精	各⅛小匙
2	海膽醬（圖1）	1½大匙
	醋	⅓大匙
	醬油	⅔大匙
	酒、味精	各⅛小匙
3	芥末醬（圖2）	少許
	貝芽菜	適量

■蒟蒻絲（圖3）入開水川燙撈出，調1料置乾鍋炒乾水份。
■將調勻的2料置碗，倒入炒好的蒟蒻絲拌勻，盛容器，上置3料即可。

SHIRATAKI WITH UNI PASTE

SERVES 4

	1/2 lb. (225 g) *shirataki*
1	1/8 t. salt
	1/8 t. each: rice wine, MSG (optional)
2	1-1/2 T. *uni* paste (sea urchin, sea chestnut paste; illus. 1)
	1/3 T. rice vinegar
	2/3 T. soy sauce
	1/8 t. rice wine, MSG (optional)
3	mustard (illus. 2), as desired
	white radish sprouts (*kaiware*), as desired

■ Blanch the *shirataki* (illus. 3) briefly in boiling water and remove. Place in a frying pan with 1 (use no oil) and stir-fry until dry.
■ Stir 2 until combined. Add the stir-fried *shirataki* and stir until well mixed. Place in a serving dish. Top with 3 and serve.

珍味綠蘆筍

アスパラのたらこ風味　　4人份

■綠蘆筍取最嫩的部份，放入開水川燙1分鐘撈出漂涼，切4公分長段盛容器。

■明太子表面劃一刀（圖2），翻面將魚子刮下（圖3），拌入酒½小匙調勻，置蘆筍上即可。

□鱈魚卵（たらこ）新鮮冷藏可生食，加調味處理者（如辣味、鹹味）則稱明太子。

□此道菜可作宴會前菜，亦是下酒佳餚。

綠蘆筍‧‧‧‧‧‧‧‧‧‧‧‧‧‧‧‧‧‧‧‧‧‧‧‧‧‧‧‧‧12枝
明太子（圖1）‧‧‧‧‧‧‧‧‧‧‧‧‧‧‧‧‧‧‧‧‧‧‧ 1片

ASPARAGUS WITH COD ROE

SERVES 4

■ Use only the most tender portion of the asparagus. Blanch in boiling water for 1 minute and remove. Cool in a bowl of tap water. Cut into 1-1/2" (4 cm) pieces and place in a serving dish.

■ Make a slash on the surface of the cod roe pouch (illus. 2). Turn over and scrape off the cod roe (illus. 3). Mix in 1/2 teaspoon rice wine. Sprinkle over the top of the asparagus and serve.

□ Fresh cod roe can be kept in the refrigerator and eaten raw. Seasoned (e.g. piquant, salty) cod roe is called *tarako*.

□ This dish can be served as an appetizer at a banquet, and is also good as an accompaniment to wine.

12 stalks green asparagus
1 pouch cod roe (*tarako*; illus. 1)

本料理由七都里餐廳提供

鮭魚子拌蘿蔔泥　　イクラと大根和え　　1人份

白蘿蔔·································600公克
鮭魚子(圖1)·····················4大匙

■白蘿蔔磨泥(圖2)，並輕輕擠乾水份(圖3)，置容器。
■將鮭魚子置白蘿蔔泥上即成，亦可酌沾少許醬油配食。
□鮭魚子市售種類有淡、鹹兩種口味，可任選使用。

SALMON ROE WITH DAIKON PUREE　　SERVES 4

1-1/3 lb. (600 g) Chinese white
　radish (*daikon*)
4 T. salmon roe (illus. 1)

■ Grind the white radish into a puree (illus. 2). Gently squeeze out the excess moisture (illus. 3) and place in a serving dish.
■ Sprinkle the salmon roe over the top of the white radish puree and serve. Small dishes of soy sauce may be served on the side as a dip, if desired.
□ Both salted and unsalted salmon roe are available commercially; choose the kind you prefer.

味噌醃小黃瓜

みそ漬け

■白味噌置乾淨無水份之容器內，調1料(圖1)拌勻。

■小黃瓜以塩1小匙揉醃約2分鐘，洗淨，置陰涼處風乾水份，放入味噌醬內拌勻(圖2)，將味噌醬連同小黃瓜放入可密封的容器內(圖3)，醃漬約2～3天，即可取出洗淨切片食用。

□除小黃瓜外，嫩茄子、高麗菜、紅、白蘿蔔等均可以同法醃製。

□醃漬時間，不宜超過3天，否則蔬菜原有的汁液會流失在味噌中。

小黃瓜	⋯⋯⋯⋯⋯⋯	600公克
白味噌	⋯⋯⋯⋯⋯⋯	400公克
1	味醂	⋯⋯⋯⋯ 5大匙
	糖	⋯⋯⋯⋯ 2大匙
	醬油	⋯⋯⋯⋯ ½大匙

MISO PICKLES

■ Place the white *miso* in a clean, dry bowl. Mix 1 (illus. 1) into the *miso* until well blended.

■ Rub 1 teaspoon salt on the cucumbers and allow to set for 2 minutes. Rinse clean. Move to a cool place to air dry. Add to the *miso* paste and mix well (illus. 2). Transfer the cucumbers with *miso* to a container that can be tightly sealed (illus. 3). Allow to cure 2 to 3 days. Rinse and cut into slices before serving.

□ Tender eggplant, head cabbage, carrots, Chinese white radish, etc., can be pickled with this same method.

□ Do not allow to cure more than 3 days, or the liquid (and flavor) contained in the vegetables will escape into the *miso* paste.

1-1/3 lb. (600 g) gherkin cucumbers

14 oz. (400 g) white *miso* (soy bean paste)

1
- 5 T. *mirin* (sweet rice wine)
- 2 T. sugar
- 1/2 T. soy sauce

醃白菜

白菜の塩漬け

白菜（淨重）·························1000公克
塩································2大匙
乾海帶（5公分）·····················1塊
紅辣椒（切片）·······················1條

■將白菜切成四等份，風乾水份（圖1）撒上塩（根部多撒些塩），海帶剪成0.2公分寬細絲備用。

■備容器（不能有水份）取一份白菜舖好，撒少許紅辣椒片及海帶絲（圖2），再舖一份白菜，頭尾交錯放入（圖3），依同法全部舖好，用石頭或重物壓約2～3天。

■醃好白菜3天後須取出洗淨（否則會變酸），並用冷開水再洗一次，擠乾水份置乾淨容器（上蓋保鮮膜）或保鮮盒存放冰箱取食方便。

□亦可使用木製或陶瓷容器來做。

PICKLED CABBAGE

2-1/4 lb. (1000 g) Chinese
cabbage (net weight)
2 T. salt
1 2" (5 cm) piece dried kelp
(*kombu*)
1 small red chili pepper, sliced

■ Quarter the Chinese cabbage and air-dry (illus. 1). Sprinkle on the salt (put extra salt on the portion near the root). With a scissors, cut the kelp into 1/10" (.2 cm) wide strips. Set aside.

■ Place two quarters of the cabbage in a dry bowl, sprinkle on some red chili pepper and kelp (illus. 2), then add another two quarters of cabbage. Place the large end of one cabbage quarter together with the small end of the other (illus. 3). Follow this procedure until all of the ingredients are used up. Cover with a wooden lid slightly smaller than the mouth of the container. Place a rock or other heavy object on top as a weight and leave undisturbed 2 to 3 days.

■ After 3 days, the cabbage must be taken out and rinsed clean (otherwise it will go sour). Rinse again in cold water, squeeze out the excess water, and store in the refrigerator in a clean container with a sealable cover; or cover with plastic wrap. Serve any amount anytime.

□ A glass or ceramic bowl or a wooden container may also be used to make pickles.

牛肉壽喜燒

牛肉片	400公克	牛蒡絲	¾杯
京葱	2枝	牛油	75公克
洋葱	1只	關東風：	
豆腐	1大塊	味醂、醬油、煮出汁…各½杯	
茼蒿菜（或菠菜）	適量	糖	2～4大匙
金菇	75公克	蛋	4個
大白菜	100公克	煮出汁	1杯
蒟蒻絲（或烏龍麵）	80公克		

■京葱切斜片，洋葱切0.5公分厚片，豆腐切大塊，茼蒿菜摘除老莖，金菇切除根部，大白菜切粗塊，分別洗淨。蒟蒻放入開水川燙撈出備用。
■將牛肉片及全部備好材料置盤整齊排好。
■鍋熱入牛油待溶化，使油均勻遍佈鍋面，放入京葱片爆香，續入牛肉片略炒及適量蔬菜，並注入煮開的 1 料，將蛋打散置小碗拌勻，一面煮一面沾蛋汁食用。
■最後將煮出汁倒入，並放入蒟蒻、豆腐、茼蒿菜等材料同煮開食用，是冬季的一道佳餚。
□ 1 料湯汁可分關東風（東京口味，湯汁較多）及關西風（大阪口味，湯汁較少，祇有醬油½杯及糖適量），可隨個人喜好調味。

BEEF SUKIYAKI

SERVES 4

14 oz. (400 g) beef, thinly sliced	2-2/3 oz. (80 g) *shirataki* (or *udon* noodles)
2 large Chinese green onions	3/4 c. burdock root (*gobō*), julienned
1 onion	2-1/2 oz. (75 g) butter
1 large cake *tofu*	Kantō style sauce:
garland chrysanthemum (*shungiku*) or spinach, as desired	1/2 c. each: *mirin*, soy sauce, *dashi*
2-1/2 oz. (75 g) *enoki*	2-4 T. sugar
3-1/2 oz. (100 g) Chinese cabbage	4 eggs
	1 c. *dashi*

■ Cut the large Chinese green onions into diagonal slices, the onion into 1/4" (.5 cm) slices, and the *tofu* into large cubes. Cut off the tough and wilted portions from the garland chrysanthemum, and the tough ends from the *enoki*. Cut the Chinese cabbage into large chunks. Wash each of the ingredients separately. Blanch the *shirataki* in boiling water. Set aside.
■ Arrange the sliced beef and all of the other ingredients neatly on serving plates.
■ Heat a *sukiyaki* pot and melt the butter in it. Move the butter around with a pair of chopsticks to distribute the butter evenly over the surface. Sauté the large Chinese green onion in the butter. Add the beef slices and stir-fry briefly. Add some of the vegetables. Bring 1 to a boil and pour over the beef and vegetables. Continue to cook at the table. Break an egg into each of 4 rice bowls and beat lightly. Dip the *sukiyaki* ingredients in the egg before eating.
■ Finally, add the *dashi*, then the *shirataki*, *tofu*, greens, etc. Bring to a boil and eat. This is an excellent winter dish.
□ 1 is Kantō (Tokyo area) style sauce, with more liquid. There is also Kansai (Osaka area) style sauce, which has less liquid; it consists simply of 1/2 cup soy sauce and sugar to taste. Use the sauce you prefer.

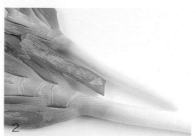

牛肉蔬菜鍋

しやぶ しやぶ　　　　4人份

嫩牛肉片(或豬肉)‥‥‥‥‥‥‥‥‥400公克
金菇‥‥‥‥‥‥75公克、鮮香菇‥‥‥‥‥4朵
大白菜‥‥‥300公克、白花菜‥‥‥‥200公克
豆腐‥‥‥‥‥‥‥‥‥‥‥‥‥‥‥‥‥1大塊
烏龍麵(或細蒟蒻)‥‥‥‥‥‥‥‥‥200公克
茼蒿菜‥‥‥‥‥‥‥‥‥‥‥‥‥‥‥‥適量

1	水‥‥‥‥‥‥‥‥‥‥‥‥‥‥‥4杯	
	乾海帶(10公分)‥‥‥‥‥‥‥‥‥1段	
2	煮出汁、醬油‥‥‥‥‥‥‥‥各¾杯	
	糖‥‥‥‥2大匙、味醂‥‥‥‥4大匙	
	味精‥‥‥‥‥‥‥‥‥‥‥‥⅛小匙	
3	芝麻粉‥‥‥‥‥‥‥‥‥‥‥‥1杯	
	白味噌‥‥‥⅛小匙、醬油‥‥‥‥¾杯	
	味醂‥‥‥‥‥‥‥‥‥‥‥‥2小匙	
4	白蘿蔔泥‥‥‥‥‥‥‥‥‥‥‥適量	
	紅辣椒末‥‥‥‥‥‥‥‥‥‥‥適量	
	檸檬汁‥‥‥‥‥‥‥‥‥‥‥⅛小匙	

■金菇切除根部洗淨,鮮香菇切斜片,白菜切粗塊,白花菜切小朵花(圖1),在開水內川燙撈起,豆腐切2公分四方塊,烏龍麵入開水川燙撈出備用。

■將牛肉片及全部材料置盤排整齊,2料、3料分別調好,4料置小碟。

■鍋入1料浸泡30分鐘後煮開,取出海帶即爲海帶汁,以筷子夾肉片在鍋內刷數次,見肉色轉白取出,依個人喜愛沾汁(2料或3料並拌入4料及檸檬汁)食用,其餘材料則邊煮邊食。

□3料內之芝麻粉做法可參考第43頁芝麻泥拌菠菜,如不喜味噌醬亦可改用芥末醬。

□京葱(圖2)可依喜好選用加入,味道更鮮美。

□以桔子(圖3)擠汁代替檸檬汁亦別具風味。

BEEF AND VEGETABLE CHAFING DISH (Shabu Shabu)
SERVES 4

14 oz. (400 g) tender beef (or pork), thinly sliced
2-1/2 oz. (75 g) *enoki*
4 fresh Chinese black mushrooms (*shiitake*)
2/3 lb. (300 g) Chinese cabbage
7 oz. (200 g) fresh cauliflower
1 large cake *tofu*
7 oz. (200 g) *udon* noodles (or fine *shirataki*)
garland chrysanthemum (*shungiku*), as desired

1
4 c. water
1 4" (10 cm) piece dried kelp (*kombu*)

2
3/4 c. each: *dashi*, soy sauce
2 T. sugar
4 T. *mirin*
1/8 t. MSG (*ajinomoto;* optional)

3
1 c. sesame seed powder
1/8 t. white *miso*
3/4 c. soy sauce
2 t. *mirin*

4
Chinese white radish (*daikon*) puree, as desired
minced fresh red chili pepper, as desired
1/8 t. lemon juice

■ Cut off the tough ends from the *enoki* and wash. Slice the mushrooms diagonally. Cut the cabbage into chunks and the cauliflower into flowerets (illus. 1). Blanch the cauliflower briefly in boiling water. Cut the *tofu* into 3/4" (2 cm) cubes. Immerse the *udon* noodles in boiling water briefly, remove, and set aside.

■ Arrange all the above ingredients, including the sliced beef, neatly on serving plates. Mix 2 and 3 separately until blended. Place 4 in a small serving dish.

■ Put 1 in a pot over a table burner, and allow to soak 30 minutes. Bring to a boil, then remove the kelp. Immerse the meat in the kelp stock and swish around a few times. Remove when the color changes. Cook the other ingredients in the stock as you eat. Dip in the sauce you prefer (2 or 3, with 4 and lemon juice stirred in) before eating.

□ See page 43, Spinach with Sesame Paste, for instructions on how to make the sesame seed powder in 3. If you do not care for *miso*, mustard may be used as a substitute.

□ Large Chinese green onion (illus. 2) may be added to the chafing dish for extra flavor.

□ Substitute freshly-squeezed kumquat (illus. 3) juice for the lemon juice for a taste variation.

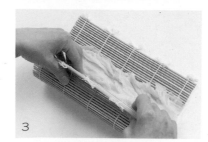

海鮮蔬菜鍋

寄せなべ　　　　　　　　4人份

新鮮魚 1 條	………………	450公克
花枝 1 隻	………………	300公克
蝦4條	………………	225公克
雞肉	………………	225公克
豆腐	………………	1 大塊
白菜	………………	600公克
紅蘿蔔	………………	¼條
菠菜	………………	1 棵

	煮出汁	………	5 杯
1	味醂	………	3 大匙
	淡口醬油	………	6 大匙
	檸檬汁	………	3 大匙
2	醬油	………	4 大匙
	煮出汁	………	1 ¾ 杯

■新鮮魚取頭，去骨（參考第8頁），魚肉切小塊，花枝切花刀（圖1）蝦背去殼，雞肉切塊，豆腐切2公分四方塊。

■白菜葉一片片取下，紅蘿蔔切0.5公分厚粗條，菠菜整棵不切，分別洗淨，以開水燙軟，取白菜葉置竹簾，上置紅蘿蔔、菠菜捲成筒狀（圖2、3），切3公分長段。

■砂鍋入1料煮開，放入魚頭、雞肉等全部材料，沾2料食用。

□亦可加入京葱、香菇、茼蒿菜等邊煮邊食。

SEAFOOD AND VEGETABLE CHAFING DISH

SERVES 4

1 fresh fish (1 lb. or 450 g)
1 cuttlefish or squid (2/3 lb. or 300 g)
4 shrimp (1/2 lb. or 225 g)
1/2 lb. (225 g) chicken meat
1 large cake *tofu*
1-1/3 lb. (600 g) Chinese cabbage
1/4 large carrot
1 bunch spinach

	5 c. *dashi*
1	3 T. *mirin*
	6 T. light-colored soy sauce
	3 T. lemon juice
2	4 T. soy sauce
	1-3/4 c. *dashi*

■ Remove the head and bones from the fish (see p. 8). Cut the fish meat into small pieces. Score the cuttlefish with a crosscut (illus. 1). Remove the shell from the body portion of the shrimp. Cut the chicken into pieces, and the *tofu* into 3/4″ (2 cm) cubes.

■ Pull the leaves off the Chinese cabbage, one by one. Cut the carrot into matchstick-sized strips. Leave the bunch of spinach whole; do not cut. Wash each ingredient thoroughly, then blanch separately in boiling water until soft. Place some cabbage leaves, carrot, and spinach on a bamboo *sushi* mat, and roll tightly into a cylinder shape (illus. 2, 3). Cut into 1-1/4″ (3 cm) pieces.

■ Add 1 to a clay pot and bring to a boil. Place the fish head, chicken meat, and the rest of the ingredients into the pot. Cook at the table while eating. Dip in 2 before eating.

□ Large Chinese green onion, dried Chinese black mushrooms, garland chrysanthemum (*shungiku*), and so forth, may also be used in this recipe.

1

2

3

關東煮

おでん　4人份

竹輪（圖1）··············	2條	
蒟蒻··················	1塊	
白蘿蔔················	300公克	
魚丸、鵪蛋·············	各12個	
海帶卷················	8卷	
油豆腐················	4塊	
牛蒡天婦羅（圖2）········	8片	
1	煮出汁···········	5杯
	味醂·············	½杯
	醬油·············	1½大匙
2	白味噌、糖·········	各2大匙
	番茄醬、冷開水······	各4大匙
	辣椒醬···········	1小匙
芥茉醬················	適量	

■竹輪切段或切斜片，蒟蒻切小塊，白蘿蔔切滾刀塊，魚丸、鵪蛋用竹簽每4個串一串備好（圖3）。

■將海帶卷入鍋川燙約2分鐘，去除腥味，另水開再放入白蘿蔔煮約5分鐘至熟撈出。

■備砂鍋一只，煮開1料，並將全部材料放入燒開後，改小火續煮約40分鐘至熟透入味，沾2料或芥末醬食用。

□此道菜的材料好壞，可決定其美味，所以必須選用上好材料，亦可以白菜捲、福袋、鱆魚等來代替使用。

TOKYO STYLE STEW (Oden)
SERVES 4

2 fried fish sausages (*chikuwa*; illus. 1)
1 cake *konnyaku*
2/3 lb. (300 g) Chinese white radish (*daikon*)
12 each: fish balls, quail eggs
8 rolls kelp (*kombu*)
4 cakes deep-fried *tofu*
8 slices burdock root (*gobō*) *tempura* (illus. 2)

1	5 c. *dashi*
	1/2 c. *mirin*
	1-1/2 T. soy sauce
2	2 T. each: white *miso*, sugar
	4 T. each: ketchup, cold water
	1 t. chili paste

mustard, as desired

■ Cut the fried fish sausages into chunks or diagonal slices. Cut the *konnyaku* into small pieces. Roll-cut the white radish into chunks. Skewer the fish balls and quail eggs, four per bamboo skewer (illus. 3).

■ Blanch the kelp rolls in boiling water for about 2 minutes to remove the seawater odor. Cook the white radish in a fresh pot of boiling water until done, about 5 minutes. Remove.

■ Bring 1 to a boil in a clay pot. Add the other ingredients to the boiling liquid, then lower the heat and simmer about 40 minutes, until the flavors are well absorbed. Dip in 2 or mustard before eating.

□ The success of this dish depends on the quality and freshness of the ingredients used. Choose the very best ingredients when shopping for this dish. Stuffed *tofu* pockets, octopus, and so forth, may be substituted for some of the ingredients in this dish.

本料理由七都里餐廳提供

1

2

3

酥炸海鮮
天ぷら盛り合わせ　　4人份

明蝦(長15公分)⋯⋯⋯⋯⋯⋯⋯8條
沙梭魚(長12公分)⋯⋯⋯⋯⋯⋯4條
花枝(淨肉)⋯⋯⋯⋯⋯⋯⋯⋯75公克
麵粉⋯⋯⋯⋯⋯⋯⋯⋯⋯⋯⋯2大匙

1
蛋(大)⋯⋯⋯⋯⋯⋯⋯⋯⋯⋯1個
冰水⋯⋯⋯⋯⋯⋯⋯⋯⋯⋯¾杯
低筋麵粉⋯⋯⋯⋯⋯⋯⋯⋯⋯1杯

三葉(圖1)⋯⋯⋯⋯⋯⋯⋯⋯⋯適量
香菇⋯⋯⋯⋯⋯⋯⋯⋯⋯⋯⋯4朵

2
味醂、醬油⋯⋯⋯⋯⋯⋯⋯各¼杯
煮出汁⋯⋯⋯⋯⋯⋯⋯⋯⋯⋯1杯
柴魚片⋯⋯⋯⋯⋯⋯⋯⋯⋯5公克

3
白蘿蔔泥⋯⋯⋯⋯⋯⋯⋯⋯⋯1杯
薑泥⋯⋯⋯⋯⋯⋯⋯⋯⋯⋯1大匙
葱花⋯⋯⋯⋯⋯⋯⋯⋯⋯⋯½枝
檸檬⋯⋯⋯⋯⋯⋯⋯⋯⋯⋯½個
七味辣粉、紅辣椒泥⋯⋯⋯⋯各少許

■蝦處理法請參考第82頁天井飯。沙梭魚洗淨去頭，由背部下刀取肉，至腹部不能切斷，反面依同法取出魚骨(參考第8頁)即成腹部相連的片狀，花枝切塊，沾少許麵粉備用。

■將1料(圖2)內的蛋加冰水調勻，麵粉過篩加入輕輕拌勻(圖3)，立即使用，以免生筋，即爲蛋糊。

■淨油2杯燒九分熱，蝦沾蛋糊一次一隻入鍋炸酥約2分鐘即撈出(炸時手沾蛋糊，滴數滴在蝦肉上，可使蝦姿更美，油面浮渣亦應撈出，油才不會變黑)，三葉、香菇沾蛋糊炸酥約1分鐘，沙梭魚、花枝亦分別沾蛋糊炸酥約3分鐘，排整齊置容器，趁熱沾2料(預先煮開過濾)食用，喜食3料者可酌量選用拌入。

□此道菜配上炸好的蔬菜即爲綜合天婦羅。

SEAFOOD TEMPURA

SERVES 4

8 large prawns (6" or 15 cm long)
4 smelt (*kisu*; 4-3/4" or 12 cm long)
2-1/2 oz. (75 g) cuttlefish or squid (net weight)
2 T. flour

1
1 large egg
3/4 c. ice water
1 c. low-gluten flour

trefoil (*mitsuba*; illus. 1), as desired
4 dried Chinese black mushrooms (*shiitake*)

2
1/4 c. each: *mirin*, soy sauce
1 c. *dashi*
1/6 oz. (5 g) bonito shavings (*katsuobushi*)

3
1 c. Chinese white radish (*daikon*) puree
1 T. ginger root puree
1/2 green onion, chopped
1/2 lemon
seven-flavor seasoning (*shichimi-tōgarashi*), red chili pepper puree, as desired

■ See page 82, Fried Shrimp over Rice *(Tendon)*, for instructions on how to prepare the shrimp. Wash the smelt and remove the head. To remove the fillet, cut from the back to the belly portion; do not cut off the meat. Turn the fish over and repeat the same procedure to remove the bones (see p. 8). You will have a fillet in one piece joined at the belly. Cut the cuttlefish into pieces and dredge in a small amount of flour. Set aside.

■ Mix the egg and water in 1 (illus. 2) until well blended. Sift the flour and slowly stir into the egg mixture to make the batter (illus. 3). Use as soon as possible so that the gluten in the flour does not become rubbery.

■ Heat 2 cups of unused vegetable oil to just under smoking. Dip the shrimp in the batter and fry in the oil one by one until crisp, about 2 minutes. When frying, dip your hand into the batter, and let a few drops drip onto the frying shrimp; this makes them more attractive. Remove any bits of batter floating in the oil, to prevent the oil from becoming black. Dip the trefoil and mushrooms in the batter and deep-fry until crisp, about 1 minute. Dip the smelt and cuttlefish in the batter and deep-fry separately, about 3 minutes each. Arrange neatly on serving plates. Serve hot with 2 as a dip on the side (boil and strain before use). Those who like the ingredients in 3 may mix some into the 2 dip.

□ This dish becomes "Assorted *Tempura*" if served with batter-fried vegetables.

本料理由七都里餐廳提供

1

2

3

酥炸羅漢齋
野菜天ぷら　　　　　　　　　　4人份

蓮藕	···························	1 節
南瓜(或蕃薯)	···················	8 片
四季豆	·························	8 條
香菇(泡軟)	·····················	4 朵
玉米筍(或黃秋葵)	·············	8 條
蘆筍	···························	8 條
茄子	···························	1 條
牛蒡絲	·························	40公克

1	蛋(大) ·························	1 個
	冰水 ·························	¾ 杯
	低筋麵粉 ·····················	1 杯
	麵粉 ·························	適量

2	味醂、醬油 ···············	各¼ 杯
	煮出汁 ·····················	1 杯
	柴魚片 ·····················	5公克

| 3 | 白蘿蔔泥 ····················· | 1 杯 |
| | 薑泥 ························· | 1 大匙 |

■ 蓮藕切0.5公分厚片,順穴邊緣修飾出花樣(圖1),其餘蔬菜材料亦分別修飾整齊(圖2、3),1料預先調好成蛋糕備用(參考第60頁酥炸海鮮)。

■ 淨油2杯燒八分熱,將蔬菜先沾乾麵粉再分別沾裹蛋糕,入鍋炸酥約3分鐘至熟,撈出盛容器,趁熱沾2、3料食用(同酥炸海鮮)

□ 炸天婦羅時油溫極為重要,可用麵糊來試溫,鍋熱後滴入少許麵糊若能迅速浮上鍋面,表示油溫約為九分熱,最適合炸海鮮,若未能迅速浮起,表示油溫稍低,約為八分熱,可用來炸蔬菜類。

□ 油炸食物炸時油溫須保持相同,炸熟後再回鍋炸30秒(將外皮的油份炸出,較酥脆)撈出。

VEGETABLE TEMPURA
SERVES 4

1 link lotus root (*renkon*)
8 slices pumpkin (or sweet potato)
8 string beans
4 dried Chinese black mushrooms (*shiitake*; soaked until soft)
8 cobs baby corn (or 8 slices okra)
8 stalks asparagus
1 eggplant (preferably long thin Oriental)
1-1/3 oz. (40 g) shredded burdock root (*gobō*)

1　1 large egg
　3/4 c. ice water
　1 c. low-gluten flour
　flour, as needed

2　1/4 c. each: *mirin*, soy sauce
　1 c. *dashi*
　1/6 oz. (5 g) bonito shavings (*katsuobushi*)

3　1 c. Chinese white radish (*daikon*) puree
　1 T. ginger root puree

■ Cut the lotus root into 1/4″ (.5 cm) slices, then carve the edges to form a decorative pattern (illus. 1). Cut the remaining vegetable ingredients into decorative patterns as well (illus. 2, 3). Mix 1 to make the batter (see p. 60, Seafood Tempura).

■ Heat 2 cups unused oil to somewhat under smoking. Dip the vegetables first in the dry flour, then in the egg batter, and deep-fry one at a time until crisp, about 3 minutes. Remove from the oil and arrange in a serving dish. Serve hot. Dip in 2 and 3 before eating (the same as with seafood *tempura*).

□ The temperature of the oil is extremely important when frying *tempura*. After heating the oil, drip a little batter in it to test the temperature; if the batter floats up quickly to the surface, the oil is about right for frying seafood *tempura*. If the batter drops do not rise as quickly to the surface, the oil is probably about the right temperature for frying vegetable *tempura*.

□ The temperature of the oil must be kept constant. After deep-frying the *tempura*, return to the oil to fry another 30 seconds for a crispier batter coating.

酥炸柳肉

ヒレとんかつ　　　4人份

豬柳肉‥‥‥‥‥‥‥‥‥‥‥‥450公克
1 ┃ 塩‥‥‥‥‥‥‥‥‥‥‥‥‥‥⅛小匙
　 ┃ 胡椒粉‥‥‥‥‥‥‥‥‥‥‥‥⅛小匙
低筋麵粉‥‥‥‥‥‥‥‥‥‥‥‥‥¼杯
蛋(打散)‥‥‥‥‥‥‥‥‥‥‥‥‥1個
麵包粉‥‥‥‥‥‥‥‥‥‥‥‥‥‥1杯
高麗菜絲‥‥‥‥‥‥‥‥‥‥‥‥‥2杯
番茄‥‥‥‥‥‥‥‥‥‥‥‥‥‥‥1個
小黃瓜(切斜薄片)‥‥‥‥‥‥‥‥1條

■ 豬柳肉切除四周白筋(圖1),分切成四等份(圖2),撒上1料並按順序輕輕沾上麵粉、蛋汁及麵包粉。

■ 鍋入油2杯燒七分熱,放入肉塊炸約5分鐘(油面浮渣應撈除乾淨),待表面呈金黃色皮酥肉熟時,撈起切塊盛盤,高麗菜絲、番茄、小黃瓜片置旁配食,食時沾上番茄醬或胡椒塩,亦可淋入少許檸檬汁。

□ 麵包粉使用前先噴少許水(圖3),炸出的皮才不會太硬。

FRIED PORK CUTLET

SERVES 4

1 lb. (450 g) pork cutlet
1 ┃ 1/8 t. salt
　 ┃ 1/8 t. pepper
1/4 c. low-gluten flour
1 egg (lightly beaten)
1 c. fine bread crumbs
2 c. shredded cabbage
1 tomato
1 gherkin cucumber (cut into thin diagonal slices)

■ Cut off the sinews from the edges of the pork cutlet (illus. 1). Cut into 4 equal pieces (illus. 2). Sprinkle on 1. Gently dip first in the flour, then in the egg mixture, then in the fine bread crumbs.

■ Heat 2 cups oil to medium hot in a frying pan or wok. Fry the cutlets about 5 minutes (be sure to remove particles from the oil when frying to keep it clean). The surface of the cutlet should be crisp and golden brown, and the meat should be cooked through. Remove from the oil, cut into pieces, and arrange in a serving dish. Garnish with the shredded cabbage, tomato, and gherkin cucumber slices. Dip in ketchup or pepper-salt before eating; or a little lemon juice may be squeezed over the top.

□ Spray the fine bread crumbs lightly with water before use (illus. 3) to prevent the fried batter coating from becoming too hard.

南蠻鯵魚

あじの南蛮漬け　　　4人份

■鯵魚（圖1）洗淨，拭乾水份（圖2）沾麵粉（圖3）備用。
■鍋入油燒熱，放入鯵魚以大火炸1分鐘後改中火慢慢炸酥（約8分鐘）撈起盛盤。
■洋葱絲入鍋炒軟，加1料煮開後，入青椒絲、紅辣椒絲一起拌勻淋在魚上，並酌量淋上檸檬汁即可供食。
□除鯵魚外，可用其他同大小的新鮮魚代替。

鯵魚4條	⋯⋯⋯⋯⋯⋯	450公克
低筋麵粉⋯⋯2大匙、炸油	⋯⋯⋯	4杯
洋葱（切絲）	⋯⋯⋯⋯⋯⋯⋯	½個
1	白醋⋯⋯⋯⋯⋯⋯⋯⋯⋯⋯	½杯
	砂糖、醬油⋯⋯⋯⋯⋯⋯各1大匙	
	煮出汁⋯⋯⋯⋯⋯⋯⋯⋯	2大匙
青椒（切絲）	⋯⋯⋯⋯⋯⋯⋯	1個
紅辣椒（切絲）	⋯⋯⋯⋯⋯	½條
檸檬	⋯⋯⋯⋯⋯⋯⋯⋯⋯⋯	½個

MACKEREL BARBARIAN STYLE

SERVES 4

■ Wash the mackerel (illus. 1) and dry with paper towels (illus. 2). Dredge in flour (illus. 3) and set aside.
■ Heat the 4 cups oil in a frying pan or wok. Deep-fry the fish in the oil over high heat for one minute. Turn the heat to medium and continue to fry until crisp (about 8 minutes). Remove from the oil and place on a serving plate.
■ Stir-fry the onion until soft. Add 1 and bring to a boil. Add the green pepper and red chili pepper, mixing well. Pour over the fish. Squeeze a little lemon juice over the top before eating.
□ Other fresh fish of a similar size may be cooked in this way.

4 mackerel (total 1 lb. or 450 g)
2 T. low-gluten flour
4 c. oil for frying
1/2 onion, cut in half-rings
1 ｜ 1/2 c. rice vinegar
1 T. each: sugar, soy sauce
2 T. *dashi*
1 green pepper, cut in julienne strips
1/2 small red chili pepper, cut in julienne strips
1/2 lemon

炸汁豆腐

揚げだし豆腐　　4人份

嫩豆腐	………………………………………	2大塊
低筋麵粉	…………………………………	½杯
白蘿蔔泥	…………………………………	½杯
薑泥	………………………………………	1大匙
蔥花	………………………………………	2大匙
味酥	……………………………………	¼杯
1　醬油	…………………………………	¼杯
煮出汁	……………………………………	1杯

■嫩豆腐切去硬邊（圖1）每塊分切4小塊（圖2），並逐塊沾上麵粉（圖3）。

■鍋熱入油3杯，燒至八分熱，將豆腐以大火炸約1分鐘呈金黃色內嫩外酥時撈起。

■將白蘿蔔泥、薑泥、蔥花放在炸好的豆腐上，淋入煮開的1料即可。

DEEP-FRIED TOFU

SERVES 4

2 large cakes soft *tofu*
1/2 c. low-gluten flour
1/2 c. Chinese white radish (*daikon*) puree
1 T. ginger root puree
2 T. chopped green onion
1/4 c. *mirin* (sweet rice wine)
1　1/4 c. soy sauce
1 c. *dashi*

■ Trim off the hard edges from the *tofu* (illus. 1) and cut each cake into 4 pieces (illus. 2). Dredge each piece in flour (illus. 3)

■ Heat a frying pan or wok and add 3 cups oil. Heat until somewhat under smoking. Fry the *tofu* over high heat about 1 minute, until it is golden brown on the outside but still tender inside. Remove from oil.

■ Place the white radish puree, ginger root puree, and chopped green onion on top of the fried *tofu*. Bring 1 to a boil, pour over the top, and serve.

本料理由七都里餐廳提供

1

2

3

基本卷壽司

基本巻きすし　　　　　　　　4人份

香菇‥‥‥‥‥‥‥‥‥‥‥‥‥‥‥4朵
1 ┌ 香菇水‥‥‥‥‥‥‥‥‥‥‥‥1杯
　├ 砂糖‥‥‥‥‥‥‥‥‥‥‥‥2大匙
　└ 醬油‥‥‥‥‥‥‥‥‥‥‥1½大匙
干瓢‥‥‥‥‥‥‥‥‥‥‥‥‥20公克
塩‥‥‥‥‥‥‥‥‥‥‥‥‥‥‥少許
2 ┌ 煮出汁‥‥‥‥‥‥‥‥‥‥‥1杯
　├ 醬油‥‥‥‥‥‥‥‥‥‥‥‥2大匙
　└ 砂糖‥‥‥‥‥‥‥‥‥‥‥‥3大匙
蛋‥‥‥‥‥‥‥‥‥‥‥‥‥‥‥4個
3 ┌ 塩、糖‥‥‥‥‥‥‥‥‥各½小匙
　└ 醬油‥‥‥‥‥‥‥‥‥‥‥⅓小匙
小黃瓜(或菠菜)‥‥‥‥‥‥‥‥‥2條
竹簾‥‥‥‥‥‥‥‥‥‥‥‥‥‥1付
紫菜(烤好的)‥‥‥‥‥‥‥‥‥‥5張
4 ┌ 水‥‥‥‥‥‥‥‥‥‥‥‥‥1杯
　└ 白醋‥‥‥‥‥‥‥‥‥‥‥‥2大匙
壽司飯‥‥‥‥‥‥‥‥‥‥‥‥4½杯

■香菇泡軟加1料煮至汁收乾，待涼切條狀。

■干瓢泡水約10分鐘，取出加塩揉洗(圖1)再調2料煮至汁收乾待涼，切與紫菜同長短備用。

■蛋打散調入3料拌勻煎成3公分厚片(參考第33頁煎卷蛋)切條，小黃瓜切4等份長條去籽備用。

■竹簾(洗淨、風乾)上置紫菜，雙手沾4料，取壽司飯1杯置中央均勻舖平，前端留1公分，另一端留2公分，將上述各項材料排在飯中央(圖2)，提起前端紫菜對向另一端的白飯(圖3)壓緊，並用竹簾捲好固定，兩頭壓緊，取下竹簾，切對半再分切8小塊(切時刀須沾濕布，才不黏刀)即成。

□家庭製作時，量少可將干瓢、香菇加上1、2料同煮至汁收乾較為簡便。

□可將紫菜改用蛋皮，飯上舖生菜，內餡隨意變化使用蝦、蘆筍、烤鰻魚等來做各種不同造型的花壽司。

BASIC ROLLED SUSHI (Norimaki)
SERVES 4

4 dried Chinese black mushrooms
　(shiitake)
1 ┌ 1 c. soak water from dried mushrooms
　├ 2 T. sugar
　└ 1-1/2 T. soy sauce
2/3 oz. (20 g) dried gourd shavings
　(kampyō)
dash of salt
2 ┌ 1 c. dashi
　├ 2 T. soy sauce
　└ 3 T. sugar
4 eggs
3 ┌ 1/2 t. each: salt, sugar
　└ 1/3 t. soy sauce
2 gherkin cucumbers (or some
　spinach)
1 bamboo sushi mat (sudare)
5 sheets purple laver (nori; toasted)
4 ┌ 1 c. water
　├ 2 T. rice vinegar
　└ 4-1/2 c. sushi rice

■ Soak the dried mushrooms until soft. Add 1 and cook until the sauce is almost completely reduced. Allow to cool, then cut the mushrooms into strips.

■ Soak the dried gourd shavings in water for about 10 minutes. Remove and rub with salt (illus. 1). Cook in 2 until the sauce is almost completely reduced. Cool and cut into pieces about the same length as the purple laver. Set aside.

■ Beat the eggs lightly and mix in 3. Fry into 1-1/4" (3 cm) thick slices (see p. 33, Japanese Egg Roll). Cut into strips. Quarter the gherkin cucumber lengthwise and scoop out the seeds. Set aside.

■ Wash the bamboo mat and air-dry. Place a sheet of purple laver on the mat. Wet both hands with 4. Pick up 1 cup of sushi rice and place in the center of the purple laver, then spread it evenly over the seaweed. Leave 3/8" (1 cm) of the seaweed free at the front, and 3/4" (2 cm) at the back. Arrange the above ingredients neatly across the center of the rice (illus. 2). Pick up the front of the seaweed (illus. 3) to roll the sushi into a cylindrical shape. Roll and press together tightly with the bamboo mat. Press even the two ends of the sushi, then remove the bamboo mat. Cut the sushi in half, then into a total of eight small pieces (wipe the knife with a wet cloth to prevent sticking). Serve.

□ When making small amounts of sushi at home, the dried gourd shavings and dried mushrooms can be cooked together in 1 and 2 until the sauce is reduced. This method saves time and bother.

□ Egg fried into a thin "pancake" may be substituted for the purple laver. Place some lettuce on top of the rice. Shrimp, asparagus, broiled eel, and so forth can be included in the filling to make all sorts of sushi variations.

綜合生魚片握壽司

鮪魚肉‥‥‥‥‥‥5片75公克			花枝肉(切薄片)‥‥3片30公克	
鯛魚肉‥‥‥‥‥‥3片45公克			熟草蝦(參考第46頁黃瓜捲大蝦)‥‥‥‥‥‥‥‥3隻	
1	水‥‥‥‥‥‥‥‥‥‥1杯		2	蛋卷(參考第33頁煎卷蛋)3片
	醋‥‥‥‥‥‥‥‥‥2大匙			血蚶、鳥貝‥‥‥‥各3個
壽司飯‥‥‥4杯・山葵醬‥‥適量			水針魚肉2片‥‥‥‥30公克	
鮭魚卵、鮮海膽‥‥‥‥各10公克			甜酸薑、檬檬片‥‥‥各適量	
紫菜(2.5公分×18公分)‥‥2張				

生魚片握壽司握法：魚肉切片法參考第9頁。
■雙手沾1料，右手取一個壽司飯(約20公克)，輕輕握緊成長方形。
■左手取魚片，中央塗上少許山葵醬(圖1)，再將壽司飯置其上(圖2)，右手食指輕壓壽司飯(圖3)，反面使魚片朝上，以右手大姆指及食指輕壓兩側使略成長形(圖4)，再用右手食指及中指輕按魚片，同時左手姆指壓住一端使魚片呈半圓的弧度(圖5)，再轉至另一端，同法反覆做2次。2料做法相同。
鮭魚卵握壽司做法：取一個壽司飯，做成長圓形，外圍以紫菜圈起，缺口處用醋沾黏，飯上填滿鮭魚卵即可。鮮海膽做法亦同。
□取食方法：壽司用筷子翻轉使飯朝上(圖6)，再沾醬油(圖7)，亦可用手取食，肉在下方，飯在上方，沾醬油(圖8)後即可入口。

ASSORTED PRESSED SUSHI WITH SASHIMI

24 PIECES

1	5 slices fresh tuna (*maguro*) fillet (2-1/2 oz. or 75 g)		2	3 thin slices cuttlefish (1 oz. or 30 g)
	3 slices fresh porgy fillet (1-2/3 oz. or 45 g)			3 cooked shrimp (see p. 46, Shrimp-Cucumber Rolls)
	1 c. water			3 slices egg roll (see p. 33, Japanese Egg Roll)
	2 T. rice vinegar			3 ark shells (*akagai*)
	4 c. *sushi* rice			3 cockles (*torigai*)
	wasabi, as desired			2 slices halfbeak (*sayori*) fillet (1 oz. or 30 g)
	1/3 oz. (10 g) fresh salmon roe			pickled sweet-sour ginger root and lemon slices, as desired
	2 strips purple laver (*nori*; 1"×5" or 2.5×18 cm)			
	1/3 oz. (10 g) fresh sea urchin (*uni*)			

How to prepare fish for pressed *sushi* with *sashimi*: Slice the fish (see p.9).
■ Dip your hands in 1. Pick up about 2/3 oz. (20 g) *sushi* rice with your right hand, and gently squeeze into a rectangular block.
■ Pick up a slice of fish in your left hand and brush a little *wasabi* over the center (illus. 1). Place the *sushi* rice block on top of it (illus. 2). Press down gently on the *sushi* rice with your right index finger (illus. 3), then turn it over so the fish is on the top. With your right thumb and index finger, press both sides so that it is roughly rectangular (illus. 4), then gently press down on the fish slice with your right index finger and middle finger. At the same time, press the fish out toward one end with your left thumb, so that the fish arcs outward (illus. 5). Turn the *sushi* around and repeat on the other end. Repeat the whole procedure on the same two ends for a finished look. Repeat the same procedure for each of the items in 2.
To make pressed *sushi* with salmon roe: Pick up a half-handful of *sushi* rice and form it into a cylindrical shape. "Frame" the rice by pressing a strip of purple laver around the outer edge; seal the two ends together onto the rice with some rice vinegar. Fill with salmon roe. Follow the same procedure for the sea urchin.
■ Arrange the assorted pressed *sushi* attractively in a serving dish and serve.
□ **To eat:** Using chopsticks, turn the *sushi* so that the filling side faces sideways (illus. 6), then dip in soy sauce (illus. 7). *Sushi* can also be eaten with the hands. Turn over so the topping is underneath and the rice on top; dip in soy sauce (illus. 8) and eat.

本料理由七都里餐廳提供

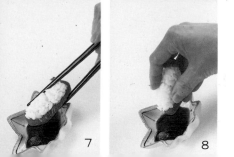

7

8

紫菜手巻
パーティ手巻すし　　6巻

	紫菜(25公分×9公分)‥‥‥‥‥‥6张	
1	生菜‥‥‥‥‥‥‥‥‥‥‥2葉	
	綠蘆筍‥‥‥‥‥‥‥‥‥‥4枝	
	熟蝦‥‥‥‥‥‥‥‥‥‥‥2條	
	柴魚片(小)‥‥‥‥‥‥‥½包	
	沙拉醬‥‥‥‥‥‥‥‥‥‥適量	
2	生菜‥‥‥‥‥‥‥‥‥‥‥2葉	
	小黄瓜(切7公分長)‥‥‥½條	
	壽司飯‥‥‥‥‥‥‥‥‥‥3大匙	
	山葵醬‥‥‥‥‥‥‥‥‥‥適量	
	生魚片‥‥‥‥‥‥‥‥‥‥2片	
3	生菜‥‥‥‥‥‥‥‥‥‥‥2葉	
	小黄瓜(切斜薄片)‥‥‥‥½條	
	鮭魚子‥‥‥‥‥‥‥‥‥‥4小匙	

■將1料之綠蘆筍以開水燙熟，切7公分長段，熟蝦參考第46頁黄瓜捲大蝦做法，其他材料全部備好置盤。

■取烤好的紫菜一張，將½的1料按順序放置一角捲起來（圖1、2、3）。

■將2料、3料依同樣的捲法包好，立刻食用（紫菜才不會變軟）。

□紫菜烤法：將紫菜置乾鍋或烤箱下層，烘烤約5秒鐘即可取出。也可選購市售烤好的使用。

□此道菜適合在宴會或茶會上以自助的方式待客。

HAND-ROLLED SEAWEED SUSHI (Temaki)
6 ROLLS

1
- 6 sheets purple laver (*nori*; 10″×3-1/2″ or 25×9 cm)
- 2 leaves lettuce
- 4 stalks green asparagus
- 2 cooked shrimp
- 1/2 packet fine bonito shavings (*hanagatsuo*)
- mayonaise, as desired

2
- 2 leaves lettuce
- 1/2 gherkin cucumber (cut 1-3/4″ or 7 cm long)
- 3 T. *sushi* rice
- *wasabi*, as desired
- 2 slices *sashimi*

3
- 2 leaves lettuce
- 1/2 gherkin cucumber (cut in thin diagonal slices)
- 4 t. salmon roe

■ Cook the asparagus in boiling water until done, then cut in 2-3/4″ (7 cm) pieces. See page 46, Shrimp-Cucumber Rolls, for instructions on how to prepare the shrimp. Arrange all the ingredients on plates and have ready.

■ Toast a sheet of purple laver. Place half of 1 in a corner of the seaweed, in order, and roll up (illus. 1, 2, 3).

■ Roll 2 and 3 in the same way as 1. Serve and eat immediately (to prevent the seaweed from becoming soggy).

□ To toast the purple laver: Place the seaweed in a dry frying pan or wok, or on the lower shelf of an oven. Toast about 5 seconds and remove. Pretoasted seaweed is also available commercially.

□ This dish is a good finger food for banquets or buffets.

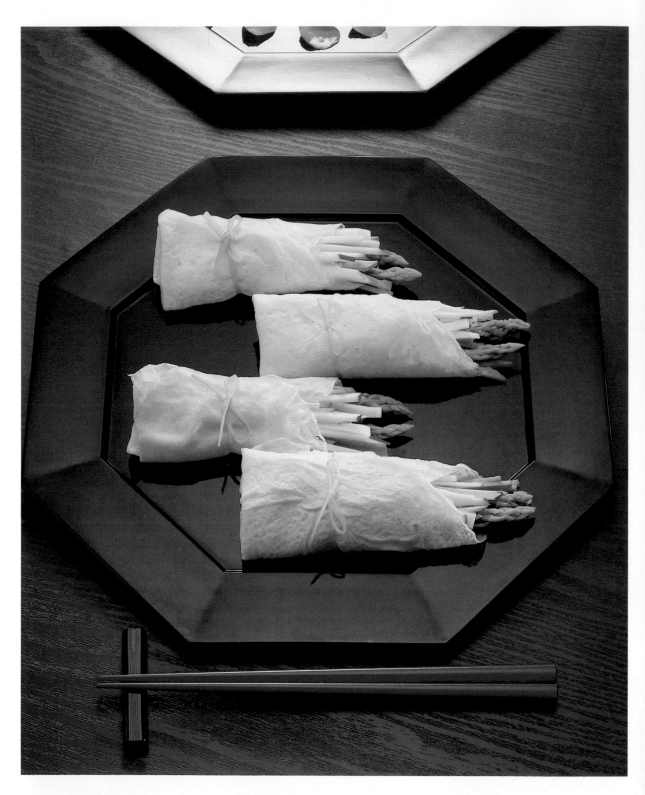

蛋皮手卷

茶巾すし　　　　４卷

綠蘆筍‥‥‥‥‥‥‥‥‥‥‥‥‥‥‥‥８枝
西洋芹菜‥‥‥‥‥‥‥‥‥‥‥‥‥‥‥½枝
蘋果‥‥‥‥‥‥‥‥‥‥‥‥‥‥‥‥‥½個
洋火腿（四方型）‥‥‥‥‥‥‥‥‥‥‥２片
芹菜‥‥‥‥‥‥‥‥‥‥‥‥‥‥‥‥‥２枝
蛋‥‥‥‥‥‥‥‥‥‥‥‥‥‥‥‥‥‥４個
生菜‥‥‥‥‥‥‥‥‥‥‥‥‥‥‥‥‥４葉
沙拉醬（或鹽）‥‥‥‥‥‥‥‥‥‥‥‥適量

■ 綠蘆筍取尾端較嫩的部分約７公分長，以開水川燙漂涼。西洋芹菜刨去筋，切７公分長段，順紋切細條，浸冰水；蘋果切細條，浸鹽水；分別瀝乾水份待用。洋火腿切細條，芹菜以開水川燙漂涼後撕成細絲。

■ 蛋打散，煎成４張蛋皮（直徑約17～20公分）。

■ 取一張蛋皮攤開，上置一片生菜葉及¼的綠蘆筍、西洋芹菜、蘋果、洋火腿及適量沙拉醬（圖１）。蛋皮對摺，材料要露出一部分（圖２），由兩端捲向中央包上，再用芹菜絲繫緊（圖３）即成。

□ 除蛋皮外，亦可用荷葉餅、吐司麵包等，將內餡包捲而食。

HAM, VEGETABLE AND EGG ROLLS

4 ROLLS

8 stalks fresh green asparagus
1/2 stalk celery
1/2 apple
2 slices ham (square)
2 stalks Chinese celery
4 eggs
4 leaves lettuce
mayonaise (or salt), as desired

■ Cut the tender ends of the green asparagus into 2-3/4″ (7 cm) lengths. Blanch in boiling water and cool in tap water. Pare off the strings from the celery and cut into 2-3/4″ (7 cm) lengths. Cut into thin strips along the grain and soak in ice water. Cut the apple into thin strips and soak in salt water. Drain each separately before use and set aside. Cut the ham into fine strips. Blanch the Chinese celery in boiling water, cool in tap water, then tear into fine strips.

■ Beat the egg lightly. Fry into 4 egg "pancakes" (about 6-1/2″ to 8″ or 17 to 20 cm in diameter).

■ Spread out one of the egg "pancakes". Lay a leaf of lettuce on it, then top with 1/4 of the asparagus, celery, apple, ham, and some mayonaise (illus. 1). Fold the egg "pancake" in half, allowing the filling to protrude somewhat (illus. 2). Roll the two ends towards the center, then secure with the Chinese celery shreds (illus. 3). Repeat for the remaining three egg "pancakes". Serve.

□ The filling ingredients can also be rolled in Chinese *moo shu* shells (Peking duck flour wrappers), bread, etc.

本料理由七都里餐廳 提供

什錦散壽司
ちらしすし　　　　1人份

壽司飯‥‥‥‥‥‥‥‥‥‥‥‥‥1杯
紫菜(剪細絲)‥‥‥‥‥‥‥‥‥‥½張
鱖魚肉‥‥‥‥‥‥‥‥‥‥‥‥‥4片
花枝‥‥‥‥‥‥‥‥‥‥‥‥‥‥2片
小黃瓜‥‥‥‥‥‥‥‥‥‥‥‥‥1條
鮪魚肉‥‥‥‥‥‥‥‥‥‥‥‥‥2片
蛋卷‥‥‥‥‥‥‥‥‥‥‥‥‥‥2片
血蚶‥‥‥‥‥‥‥‥‥‥‥‥‥‥1個
鱆魚‥‥‥‥‥‥‥‥‥‥‥‥‥‥1片
烤鰻魚(4公分×4公分)‥‥‥‥‥‥1片
鯖魚‥‥‥‥‥‥‥‥‥‥‥‥‥‥2片
蝦‥‥‥‥‥‥‥‥‥‥‥‥‥‥‥1條
鳥貝‥‥‥‥‥‥‥‥‥‥‥‥‥‥1片
如意魚捲‥‥‥‥‥‥‥‥‥‥‥‥2塊
香菇(煮熟)‥‥‥‥‥‥‥‥‥‥‥1朵
山葵醬‥‥‥‥‥‥‥‥‥‥‥‥‥½小匙

■將壽司飯(參考第6頁)置容器，撒上紫菜絲，將鱖魚肉捲花(參考拼盤與盤飾第103頁)，花枝片攤開，中央置½條小黃瓜捲起，缺口以牙籤固定後切塊。鮪魚肉、蛋捲(參考第33頁煎卷蛋)、血蚶等全部材料亦分別整齊排好。

■將另½條小黃瓜切斜薄片，香菇放置一旁裝飾，並擺上山葵醬即可，此爲關東(東京)吃法。

□購買現成的如意魚捲使用方便，如欲自製，可取長8公分，寬4公分的魚肉切0.5公分薄片，由兩端捲向中央，使呈如意形，亦可先鋪上紫菜後再捲。

□散壽司材料可隨意增減使用，亦可分別切絲後撒在壽司飯上(圖1、2、3)，此爲關西(大阪)吃法。

□容器選用碗或木製飯盒均可。

SUSHI SALAD

SERVES 1

- 1 c. *sushi* rice
- 1/2 sheet purple laver (*nori*; cut into fine shreds)
- 4 slices marlin (*kajiki*) fillet
- 2 slices cuttlefish (*ika*)
- 1 gherkin cucumber
- 2 slices tuna fish (*maguro*) fillet
- 2 slices Japanese egg roll
- 1 ark shell (*akagai*)
- 1 slice octopus (*tako*)
- 1 slice (1-1/2″ or 4 cm square) broiled eel (*unagi*)
- 2 slices mackerel (*saba*)
- 1 shrimp
- 1 slice cockle (*torigai*)
- 2 fish rolls
- 1 dried Chinese black mushroom (*shiitake*; soaked until soft and cooked)
- 1/2 t. *wasabi* (Japanese horseradish)

■ Place the *sushi* rice (see p. 6) in a serving dish and sprinkle on the purple laver shreds. Roll the marlin into a flower (see ''Chinese Appetizers and Garnishes'', p. 103). Spread open the cuttlefish slices, place 1/2 gherkin cucumber on top, and roll up. Secure with a toothpick, then cut into pieces. Arrange the tuna fish fillet, Japanese egg roll slices (see p. 33), ark shell, and other ingredients neatly on a platter.

■ Cut the other half of the gherkin cucumber into thin diagonal slices. Place the mushroom on the side as a garnish, then top with the *wasabi* and serve. This is a Kantō (Tokyo) style dish.

□ Fish rolls can either be bought ready-made, or made yourself at home. To make: Cut a 3″×1-1/2″ (8×4 cm) piece of fish fillet into 1/8″ (.5 cm) slices. Roll both ends toward the center to form a double scroll. A strip of purple laver may be placed on top of the fish slice before it is rolled.

□ As a variation, the above ingredients may be shredded and sprinkled over the *sushi* rice (illus. 1,2,3). This is the Kansai (Osaka) version of *Sushi* Salad.

□ Serve *Sushi* Salad in a bowl or wooden rice box.

豆腐皮鑲飯

いなりすし　　　4人份

■油豆腐皮切成三角形（圖1），放入1料內煮開，改小火煮至汁收乾，待涼。

■雙手沾2料，將壽司飯鑲入油豆腐皮內約八分滿（圖2），開口處再沾上少許黑芝麻（圖3），並以酸薑絲搭配食用。

☐豆腐皮可變化切成四方型、長方型或卷型。

☐也可將冬菇丁、紅蘿蔔丁、干瓢丁加入1料內同煮至汁收乾，待涼與切碎的小黃瓜一同拌勻，鑲入壽司飯內。

☐酸薑絲做法：鮮嫩薑300公克切薄片，入水川燙1分鐘撈出浸泡糖醋汁（糖3大匙、醋3大匙）即可。

方型油豆腐皮	·10張
1 煮出汁	⅔杯
砂糖	5大匙
醬油	3大匙
2 水	1杯
白醋	2大匙
壽司飯	約4½杯
黑芝麻（炒好）	2小匙
酸薑絲	適量

TOFU POCKET SUSHI (Inarizushi)

SERVES 4

■ Cut the fried *tofu* pockets diagonally into triangles (illus. 1). Place in a pot with 1 and bring to a boil. Cook until the sauce is completely reduced, and set aside to cool.

■ Dip both hands in 2. Stuff the *tofu* pockets about 4/5 full with *sushi* rice (illus. 2). Sprinkle a little toasted black sesame seed over the top (illus. 3). Eat with the pickled shredded ginger root.

☐ The square fried *tofu* pockets can be cut into squares or rectangles, or they can be rolled, for variation.

Diced dried Chinese black mushroom (*shiitake*), diced carrot, and diced dried gourd shaving (*kampyō*) may be cooked with 1 until the sauce is reduced. Allow to cool, then mix in with the *sushi* rice, along with some chopped gherkin cucumber.

☐ To make shredded pickled ginger root: cut 2/3 lb. (300 g) fresh young ginger into thin slices, and blanch in boiling water 1 minute. Remove and pickle in 3 tablespoons sugar and 3 tablespoons vinegar.

10 square fried *tofu* pockets
1 | 2/3 c. *dashi*
5 T. sugar
3 T. soy sauce
2 | 1 c. water
2 T. rice vinegar
4-1/2 c. *sushi* rice (approx.)
2 t. toasted black sesame seeds
shredded pickled sweet-sour
ginger root, as desired

蟹肉雜炊

かに雑ぎ炊ぎ　　　4人份

蟹肉	‥‥‥‥‥‥‥‥‥‥‥‥‥	1罐
薑汁	‥‥‥‥‥‥‥‥‥‥‥‥‥	1大匙
白飯	‥‥‥‥‥‥‥‥‥‥‥‥‥	2碗
香菇	‥‥‥‥‥‥‥‥‥‥‥‥‥	2朵
菠菜	‥‥‥‥‥‥‥‥‥‥‥‥‥	4棵
1	煮出汁‥‥‥‥4杯、塩‥‥‥‥	1小匙
	淡口醬油‥‥‥‥‥‥‥‥‥‥	2小匙
	味精‥‥‥‥‥‥‥‥‥‥‥‥	少許
越前棒(仿蟹肉)	‥‥‥‥‥‥‥	75公克
蛋	‥‥‥‥‥‥‥‥‥‥‥‥‥	4個

■取蟹肉拌入薑汁(圖1)，白飯用冷水沖開成粒狀(圖2)。

■香菇泡軟切粗條，菠菜切段備用。

■燒開1料入白飯及香菇大火煮開，續入蟹肉、越前棒(圖3)、菠菜略煮，將泡沫撈出，加蛋熄火即可。

□薑汁做法：取薑磨泥後去渣取汁即成。

□依個人喜愛可加入紫菜絲、生蠔、蛤蜊、魚肉等材料。

CRAB AND RICE MIX-UP

SERVES 4

1 can crab meat
1 T. ginger root juice
2 bowls cooked rice
2 dried Chinese black mushrooms
4 bunches spinach

1
4 c. *dashi*
1 t. salt
2 t. light-colored soy sauce
pinch of MSG (optional)

2-1/2 oz. (75 g) artificial crab meat
4 eggs

■ Stir the ginger root juice into the crab meat (illus. 1). Add some cold water to the cooked rice to separate the grains (illus. 2).

■ Soak the mushrooms until soft and cut into thick strips. Cut the spinach into pieces. Set aside.

■ Bring 1 to a boil. Add the cooked rice and mushrooms and bring to a full second boil over high heat. Add the crab meat, the artificial crab meat (illus. 3), and the spinach. Cook briefly. Skim off the foam, break in the eggs and turn off the heat. Serve.

□ To make ginger root juice: filter off the liquid from ginger root puree.

□ Purple laver shreds, fresh oysters, clams, fish fillets, and so forth may be added to this dish according to individual preference.

茶汁飯

さけ茶漬け　　　4人份

■鹹鮭魚烤熟，去皮、魚骨及小刺，撕成細絲（圖3）。
■白飯置容器，撒上1料、鮭魚絲及2料，並注入熱茶即成。亦可搭配泡菜或撒上柴魚絲食用。
□茶汁用綠茶或烏龍茶均可。
□如將前餐剩餘的鹹鮭魚肉做茶汁飯，也是一道方便的簡餐。

鹹鮭魚		37公克
白飯		4碗
1	味精	⅛小匙
	塩	⅙小匙
	白芝麻（圖1）	1大匙
2	三葉	4枝
	紫菜絲	適量
	山葵醬（圖2）	1小匙
茶（汁）		3杯

TEA RICE

SERVES 4

■ Broil the salted salmon until cooked through. Skin and debone; tweeze out the fine bones. Tear into fine shreds (illus. 3).

■ Place the cooked rice in a serving dish. Top with 1, the salted salmon shreds, and 2. Pour on the hot tea and serve. Pickled vegetables may be added on the side, or top with bonito shreds.

□ Use either green or oolong tea.

□ This dish is especially convenient if you shred fried salted salmon leftover from the previous meal.

1-1/3 oz. (37 g) salted salmon (*shiojake*)

4 c. cooked rice

1 ⎰ 1/8 t. MSG (optional)
  ⎱ 1/6 t. salt
  1 T. white sesame seeds (illus. 1)

2 ⎰ 4 stalks trefoil (*mitsuba*)
  purple laver (*nori*) shreds, as desired
  1 t. *wasabi* (Japanese horseradish; illus. 2)

3 c. tea

勝丼飯

かつ丼　　4人份

里肌肉	··	400公克
	麵粉 ···	½杯
1	蛋（打散）·································	1個
	麵包粉 ······································	¾杯
白飯	···	4碗
2	煮出汁 ······ 1½杯、味酥 ······· 5大匙	
	醬油 ······ 2½大匙、砂糖 ······· 1小匙	
葱片（綠色部份）·································		適量
蛋（打散）·····································		4個

■里肌肉切1公分厚片，以刀背或搥肉器拍鬆，撒上鹽、胡椒粉各⅛小匙，按順序沾上1料（圖1、2、3）。

■炸油3杯燒熱至160℃（七分熱），將肉片投入中火炸至呈金黃色，肉熟皮酥時撈起切塊置白飯上。

■2料燒開，入葱片、蛋汁煮至半熟狀，速起鍋，淋在炸好的肉片上即成。

PORK CUTLET OVER RICE (Katsudon)

SERVES 4

> 14 oz. (400 g) lean pork
>
> 1   1/2 c. flour
>   1 egg, lightly beaten
>   3/4 c. fine bread crumbs
>
> 4 c. cooked rice
>
>   1-1/2 c. *dashi*
> 2   5 T. *mirin* (sweet rice wine)
>   2-1/2 T. soy sauce
>   1 t. sugar
>
> sliced green onion, green portion only, as desired
>
> 4 eggs, lightly beaten

■ Cut the lean pork into 3/8" (1 cm) thick slices. Tenderize by pounding with the dull edge of a cleaver or a meat mallet. Sprinkle on 1/8 teaspoon each of salt and pepper. Dip the pork slices in the ingredients in 1, in order (illus. 1, 2, 3).

■ Heat 3 cups cooking oil to 320°F (160°C). Deep-fry the pork slices over medium heat until golden brown on both sides and cooked through. Remove from the oil, cut into pieces, and place some pork in each rice-filled bowl.

■ Bring 2 to a boil. Add the green onion and egg. When the egg is about half set, pour over the pork and rice. Serve.

天丼飯

天丼　　　　4人份

■蝦去殼留尾，摘除三角刺（圖1）並切去末端（圖2），用刀背刮出蝦尾內水份。蝦腹輕切數刀（圖3）拍直備用。
■炸油2杯燒熱，蝦沾1料炸酥（參考第60頁酥炸海鮮），並把青椒茄子、芋頭等亦分別沾1料炸酥（參考第62頁酥炸羅漢齋）作爲配菜
■熱白飯盛碗，擺上炸好的蝦及蔬菜各1份，再淋上煮開的2料拌食。

蝦		···········4條	
1	低筋麵粉	½杯、蛋	½個
	水（或冰水）		⅓杯
青椒		4片、茄子	4片
芋頭		4片、白飯	4碗
2	味酥		5大匙
	砂糖		1小匙
	醬油		2½大匙
	煮出汁		1½杯

FRIED SHRIMP OVER RICE (Tendon)

SERVES 4

■ Shell the shrimp, but leave the tail intact. Remove the tips of the tails (illus. 1) and chop off the ends of the double tail shells (illus. 2). Scrape out the moisture contained in the shrimp tail with the dull edge of a knife. Make several gentle slashes in the belly portion of the shrimp (illus. 3), lightly pound it straight, and set aside.

■ Heat 2 cups cooking oil. Dip the shrimp in 1 and deep-fry until crisp (see p. 60, Seafood Tempura). Separately dip the green pepper, eggplant, and taro in 1 and fry until crisp (see p. 62, Vegetable Tempura).

■ Put 1 cup of cooked rice into each individual bowl, and top with the batter-fried shrimp and vegetables. Bring 2 to a boil, and pour some over each portion. Toss and eat.

	4 jumbo shrimp
	1/2 c. low-gluten flour
1	1/2 egg
	1/3 c. water (or ice water)
	4 slices green pepper
	4 slices eggplant
	4 slices taro (dasheen)
	4 c. cooked rice
	5 T. *mirin* (sweet rice wine)
2	1 t. sugar
	2-1/2 T. soy sauce
	1-1/2 c. *dashi*

親子飯

親子丼　　　4人份

雞腿(淨肉)	······	120公克
洋葱	······	1 個
京葱	······	2 枝
蛋	······	4 個
1	煮出汁	1½杯
	味醂	5 大匙
	砂糖	1½小匙
	醬油	2 大匙
白飯	······	4 碗

■雞腿肉切粗條(圖1),洋葱切絲(圖2),京葱切斜片(圖3)蛋打散備用。

■燒開1料,入雞肉、洋葱煮軟,續入蛋汁及京葱片,待蛋呈半熟狀即可起鍋,淋在白飯上。

CHICKEN AND EGG OVER RICE (Oyako Domburi) SERVES 4

1/4 lb. (120 g; net wt.) chicken leg (dark) meat
1 onion
2 large Chinese green onions
4 eggs

1
- 1-1/2 c. *dashi*
- 5 T. *mirin*
- 1-1/2 t. sugar
- 2 T. soy sauce

4 c. cooked rice

■ Cut the chicken meat into thick strips (illus. 1), the onion into half-rings (illus. 2), and the large Chinese green onion into diagonal slices (illus. 3). Beat the eggs lightly and set aside.

■ Bring 1 to a boil. Add the chicken and onion, and cook until soft. Next add the beaten eggs and large Chinese green onion. When the egg is about half set, pour some of the contents over each portion of rice. Serve.

牛丼飯

牛丼　　　4人份

■鍋入 1 料及洋葱片，將洋葱煮軟，續入牛肉片、葱片略煮，立即
鏟出置白飯上，並加紅嫩薑片（圖3）即成。

牛肉片（圖1）·········	······	300公克
	糖、醬油·········	····各 1 小匙
	塩·········	·····½小匙
1	煮出汁·········	···1 ½杯
	味酥········· 5 大匙、胡椒·········	½小匙
洋葱片（圖2）·········	······	1 ½杯
葱（切片）·········	······	4 枝
白飯·········	······	4 碗
紅嫩薑片·········	······	適量

BEEF OVER RICE (Gyudon)

SERVES 4

■ Add 1 and the onion to a saucepan, and cook until the onion is soft. Next add the sliced beef and green onion, and cook briefly. Put some of the contents over each rice-filled bowl, and top with some sliced pickled red ginger root (illus. 3). Serve.

2/3 lb. (300 g) sliced beef (illus. 1)

1 | 1 t. each: sugar, soy sauce
1/2 t. salt
1-1/2 c. *dashi*
5 T. *mirin*
1/8 t. pepper

1-1/2 c. sliced onion (illus. 2)
4 green onions, sliced
4 c. cooked rice
sliced pickled red ginger root (*beni-shōga*), as desired

紅豆飯

赤豆飯　　4人份

紅豆‧‧‧‧‧‧‧‧‧‧‧‧‧‧‧‧‧‧‧‧‧‧‧‧‧‧‧‧‧‧‧‧‧‧⅓杯
糯米‧‧‧‧‧‧‧‧‧‧‧‧‧‧‧‧‧‧‧‧‧‧‧‧‧‧‧‧‧‧‧‧‧‧5杯

■紅豆選顆粒大無雜質爲佳（圖1），加水2杯煮滾，將水倒出，以去苦味，另加水3杯煮開，改小火煮約30分鐘至紅豆略開（圖2），取出瀝乾，汁留用。

■糯米洗淨，泡入紅豆汁內（圖3）約8小時，瀝乾（汁留用）拌上紅豆，倒入蒸籠（蒸籠預先舖上墊布）舖平，以大火蒸約50分鐘（蒸時將紅豆汁分4～5次淋入）即成。

□紅豆飯常於佳節喜慶時食用，象徵吉祥如意。

RED BEAN RICE

SERVES 4

1/3 c. red (*adzuki, azuki*) beans
5 c. glutinous rice (sweet rice)

■ Choose red beans that are large and have no foreign matter mixed in (illus. 1). Add 2 cups water and bring to a boil. Discard the water (this is to remove any bitterness). Add a fresh 3 cups of water and again bring to a boil. Turn the heat to low and simmer about 30 minutes, until the beans begin to split open (illus. 2). Remove the beans, drain well, and retain the cooking liquid.

■ Wash the glutinous rice and soak in the liquid used to cook the red beans (illus. 3) about 8 hours. Drain well, again retaining the liquid. Mix the red beans into the glutinous rice. Transfer to a cloth-lined steamer, and spread out evenly. Steam over high heat for about 50 minutes (pour the liquid from cooking the red beans over the rice as it steaming; pour in a little at a time each of 4 to 5 separate times). Serve.

□ Red Bean Rice is often served on holidays and at celebrations; it symbolizes happiness and good fortune.

1

2

3

雙色飯

二色どんぶり　4人份

牛絞肉	225公克
1 砂糖	2大匙
醬油	4大匙
味醂	1大匙
白飯	6碗
蛋	5個
2 塩	⅓小匙
煮出汁	3大匙
糖	少許
熟青豆仁	75公克
紅嫩薑絲	少許

■鍋熱加油1小匙，入牛絞肉（圖1）炒至肉色轉白，續入1料拌炒至汁收乾，盛出置白飯上。

■蛋打散，拌入2料攪勻。

■油4大匙燒熱，倒入蛋汁拌炒至蛋凝固，盛出置牛肉旁，最後撒上青豆仁（圖2）及紅嫩薑絲（圖3）即成。

□依個人喜好，亦可加入熟香菇絲（參考第69頁基本卷壽司）及紫菜絲。

TWO COLOR RICE

SERVES 4

1/2 lb. (225 g) ground beef

1 | 2 T. sugar
| 4 T. soy sauce
| 1 T. *mirin* (sweet rice wine)

6 c. cooked rice

5 eggs

2 | 1/3 t. salt
| 3 T. *dashi*
| dash of sugar

2-1/2 oz. (75 g) cooked peas

shredded pickled red ginger root (*beni-shōga*), as desired

■ Heat a frying pan and add 1 teaspoon cooking oil. Put in the ground beef (illus. 1) and stir-fry until the meat changes color. Add 1 and continue to stir-fry until the sauce is reduced. Pour over the cooked rice.

■ Beat the eggs lightly. Mix in 2 until well blended.

■ Heat 4 tablespoons cooking oil in a frying pan, pour in the egg mixture, and stir-fry until the egg is set. Place on the rice next to the ground beef. Scatter some cooked peas (illus. 2) and shredded pickled red ginger root (illus. 3) over the top and serve.

□ Cooked dried Chinese black mushroom strips (see p. 69 Basic Rolled Sushi) and shredded purple laver (*nori*) may be added according to individual preference.

什錦飯

五目ごはん　　4人份

米	···	3杯
	雞肉	·································· 100公克
	紅蘿蔔	································· 30公克
1	油豆腐皮	····························· 1 張
	蒟蒻	··································· ¼塊
	青豆仁	····························· 1 大匙
	塩	··································· ⅓小匙
2	淡口醬油	··························· 3 大匙
	酒	································· 1 大匙
煮出汁	··	3杯
紅嫩薑絲	·····································	少許

■將１料（圖１）內之雞肉、紅蘿蔔、油豆腐皮、蒟蒻切絲及青豆仁置盆，調入２料醃約20分鐘（圖２）備用。

■米洗淨加煮出汁及全部材料拌勻（圖３）煮熟，再撒上紅嫩薑絲即成。

LITTLE-OF-EVERYTHING RICE

SERVES 4

3 c. raw rice

1 | 3-1/2 oz. (100 g) chicken meat
1 oz. (30 g) carrot
1 square fried *tofu* pocket
1/4 cake *konnyaku*
1 T. peas

2 | 1/3 t. salt
3 T. light-colored soy sauce
1 T. rice wine

3 c. *dashi*

shredded pickled red ginger root
(*beni-shōga*), as desired

■ Cut the chicken, carrot, fried *tofu* pocket, and *konnyaku* of 1 (illus. 1) into julienne strips. Place in a bowl with the peas. Mix in 2 and marinate about 20 minutes (illus. 2). Set aside.

■ Wash the rice, then add the *dashi* and all the other ingredients, and mix carefully until blended (illus. 3). Cook until done. Sprinkle on some shredded pickled red ginger and serve.

握飯

おにぎり　　　3個

■白飯分成三個小飯糰。
■鹹梅去籽，切成三小塊。
■每個飯糰包上梅肉。飯糰置左手，彎曲(圖2)，右手蓋在飯上(圖3)，依此法反覆握成三角形，分別圈上紫菜、沾滾碎海苔芝麻或黑芝麻即成。
□亦可用市售現成的模型來做更方便。

白飯	1½杯
鹹梅	1個
紫菜(15×2公分)	1張
海苔香鬆(圖1)	適量
黑芝麻	適量

RICE BALLS (Onigiri)

3 BALLS

■ Divide the rice into 3 balls.
■ Remove the seed from the pickled plum, and cut the plum into three pieces.
■ Place one piece of pickled plum in each rice ball. Place a rice ball in your left hand, and press into an angle (illus. 2); place your right hand on top of the rice ball and flatten it down (illus. 3). Repeat this process until the rice ball is in the shape of a triangle. Encircle one of the balls with a strip of purple laver; roll the second ball in the crushed laver; and roll the last one in the black sesame seeds. Serve.
□ Rice balls can also be made by pressing the rice into rice molds available commercially.

1-1/2 c. cooked rice
1 pickled plum (umeboshi)
1 strip purple laver (nori; 6″ × 3/4″ or 15×2 cm)
crushed laver (furigake; illus. 1), as desired
black sesame seeds, as desired

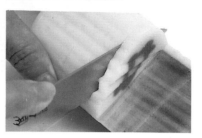

鍋燒烏龍麵

鍋焼きうどん　　　4人份

熟烏龍麵（圖1）4包		1000公克
香菇		4朵
1	泡香菇水	½杯
	砂糖 2½大匙、醬油	1大匙
魚板	½條、菠菜	4棵
雞肉		80公克
蝦	4條、蛤蜊	8個
2	煮出汁 4杯、塩	¼小匙
	味醂、淡口醬油	各½杯
蛋		4個
七味辣粉		少許

■香菇泡軟加1料煮至入味（約8分鐘），魚板以刀傾斜約15度切入並將刀左右抖動切成旭日形片狀（圖2、3），菠菜入開水川燙約30秒後撈出，擠乾水份切3公分長段，雞肉切片備用。

■熟烏龍麵以熱水川燙30秒後撈出盛砂鍋內，上置香菇、雞肉片、魚板、蝦、蛤蜊等材料，並注入2料以大火煮滾，再加蛋略煮至蛋呈半固體狀時，放入菠菜即可起鍋，趁熱供食。亦可撒少許七味辣粉。

□烏龍麵有生、乾及煮熟的，可任選使用。

UDON IN BROTH

SERVES 4

4 packages (2 lb. 3 oz. or 1000 g) precooked *udon* noodles (illus.1)

4 dried Chinese black mushrooms (*shiitake*)

1 1/2 c. mushroom soak water
2-1/2 T. sugar, 1 T. soy sauce

1/2 fish cake (*kamaboko*)

4 bunches spinach

3 oz. (80 g) chicken meat

4 shrimp, 8 clams

2 4 c. *dashi*, 1/4 t. salt
1/2 c. each: *mirin*, light-colored soy sauce

4 eggs

seven-flavor seasoning (*shichimi-tōgarashi*), as desired

■ Soak the mushrooms until soft, then cook in 1 until the flavors are well absorbed (about 8 minutes). Cut the fish cake at about a 15° angle, and alternate the knife back and forth while cutting to form a rippled rising sun pattern (illus. 2, 3). Blanch the spinach in boiling water about 30 seconds. Squeeze out the excess moisture and cut into 1-1/4″ (3 cm) lengths. Slice the chicken. Set aside.

■ Immerse the precooked *udon* noodles in hot water for 30 seconds, and transfer to a clay pot. Place the mushrooms, chicken slices, fish cake slices, shrimp, and clams on top of the noodles. Pour in 2 and bring to a boil over high heat. Pour in the egg and continue to cook until the egg is about half set. Add the spinach. Serve hot. A little seven-flavor seasoning may be sprinkled over the top, if desired.

□ *Udon* noodles are sold in fresh uncooked, dry, and cooked forms; choose the kind you prefer.

2

日式涼麺

冷しそうめん　　　4人份

日式素麵	4束
蝦(中)	4條
小黃瓜	2條
蛋	2個
魚板	8片
碎冰塊	約4杯
1　煮出汁	1杯
味醂、淡口醬油	各¼杯
柴魚絲	5公克
2　葱花	2大匙
紫菜(剪細絲)	1張
薑泥	1½大匙

■日式素麵(圖1)放入開水中煮滾，再加水1杯續煮約1分鐘至麵心熟透，撈出漂冷水，瀝乾水份(圖2)放入冰塊置冰箱冰涼。

■蝦煮熟去殼，小黃瓜切圓薄片，蛋打散煎成蛋皮，切絲備用。

■將1料煮開過濾即爲麵汁。

■備透明碗1只，放入冰塊(或冰水)，上置素麵(圖3)，並將蛋皮絲、蝦、小黃瓜、魚板依序排整齊，麵汁置小碗(約六分滿)，2料置小碟。

■取素麵沾上麵汁(汁內拌入2料)即可食用。

□日式素麵亦可改用中式麵線，配料可依個人喜好而變化。

COLD NOODLES

SERVES 4

4 bunches *sōmen* (thin wheat noodles)
4 medium shrimp
2 gherkin cucumbers
2 eggs
8 slices fish cake (*kamaboko*)
4 c. crushed ice (approx.)

1　1 c. *dashi*
　1/4 c. each: *mirin*, light-colored soy sauce
　1/6 oz. (5 g) bonito shreds

2　2 T. chopped green onion
　1 sheet purple laver, cut into thin strips
　1-1/2 T. ginger root puree

■ Place the *sōmen* (illus. 1) in boiling water. After it comes to a second boil, add 1 cup of tap water and continue to cook about 1 minute, until the noodles are cooked through. Remove from the boiling water and place in a bowl of tap water to cool. Drain (illus. 2), then add some crushed ice, and chill in the refrigerator.

■ Cook the shrimp and remove the shells. Cut the gherkin cucumber into thin rounds. Beat the egg lightly, fry into a thin egg "pancake", and cut into shreds. Set aside.

■ Bring 1 to a boil and strain. This is the broth for the cold noodles.

■ Place ice cubes (or ice water) in a transparent bowl. Add the *sōmen* (illus. 3). Arrange the egg shreds, shrimp, cucumber, and fish cake neatly on top. Divide the broth among four small bowls, filling each about 3/5 full. Place 2 in a small dish.

■ Add some of 2 into the noodle broth. Take some noodles and other ingredients and dip in the broth before eating.

□ Chinese vermicelli can be substituted for the *sōmen*, and the other ingredients can be varied according to individual preference.

2

3

玉台翡翠麵

ざるそば　　　　　　　　　　　4人份

喬麥麵	⋯⋯⋯⋯⋯⋯⋯⋯⋯⋯	4束
1	煮出汁 ⋯⋯⋯⋯⋯⋯⋯⋯⋯	1杯
	味醂 ⋯⋯⋯⋯⋯⋯⋯⋯⋯⋯	¼杯
	淡口醬油 ⋯⋯⋯⋯⋯⋯⋯	¼杯
	柴魚絲 ⋯⋯⋯⋯⋯⋯⋯⋯	5公克
2	葱花 ⋯⋯⋯⋯⋯⋯⋯⋯⋯⋯	1杯
	山葵醬 ⋯⋯⋯⋯⋯⋯⋯⋯	⅛小匙
	白蘿蔔泥 ⋯⋯⋯⋯⋯⋯⋯	½杯
	紫菜(剪成細絲) ⋯⋯⋯	1張

■喬麥麵(圖１)煮熟，浸冰水10杯冰涼，瀝乾置容器。
■１料煮開過濾置小碗即爲麵汁，２料(可加新鮮鵪蛋)分別置小碟
■取麵沾上麵汁(汁內拌入２料)即可食用。

□喬麥麵做法：喬麥的果實呈褐色，去殼後磨成粉末即可使用(圖
２)，將喬麥粉10杯加低筋麵粉２杯及塩⅛小匙，再加水約３杯，揉
成軟硬適中的麵糰，(太乾則加水，太濕加乾麵粉)醒約１小時，請
參考第７頁自製烏龍麵做法，最後切成0.2公分寬的細麵條即成。

□喬麥每年於９月～10月收成，是喬麥麵最好吃的季節，喬麥麵有
乾或新鮮的，除了冷食之外，亦可熱食，例如烏龍麵或中式的湯麵
煮法，亦別具風味。

□也可用山葵粉(圖３)調製山葵醬。其做法爲：將山葵粉用冷開水
或温開水調成濃稠狀(其比例約爲３大匙粉對1½大匙水)，置密閉容
容器約10分鐘即成。

EMERALD BUCKWHEAT NOODLES
SERVES 4

4 bunches buckwheat noodles (*soba*)

1
1 c. *dashi*
1/4 c. *mirin* (sweet rice wine)
1/4 c. light-colored soy sauce
1/6 oz. (5 g) bonito shreds

2
1 c. chopped green onion
1/8 t. *wasabi* (Japanese horseradish)
1/2 c. Chinese white radish (*daikon*) puree
1 sheet purple laver (*nori*; cut into shreds)

■ Cook the buckwheat noodles (illus. 1). Soak in 10 cups ice water to cool. Drain well and place in a serving dish.

■ Bring 1 to a boil, strain, and place in small bowls; this is the broth for the noodles. Place each of the ingredients in 2 (fresh quail eggs may also be added) in separate small dishes.

■ Mix some of 2 into the broth, then dip the noodles and other ingredients in the broth to eat.

□ How to Make Homemade Buckwheat Noodles (*Soba*): Use buckwheat with brown kernels. Remove the husks and grind into flour (illus. 2). Add 2 cups low-gluten flour, 1/8 teaspoon salt, and 3 cups water to 10 cups buckwheat flour. Knead into a smooth dough that is neither too soft nor too stiff (if the dough is too dry, add more water; if too sticky, add dry flour). Leave undisturbed about 1 hour. See page 7, How to Make Homemade Udon Noodles for instructions on rolling out the dough. Cut into 3/16″ (.2 cm) thin noodles.

□ Buckwheat is harvested during September and October, so these two months are the buckwheat noodle "season", when *soba* is at its freshest and best. *Soba* comes in dry and fresh uncooked forms. It can be eaten cold or hot; try using it in recipes calling for *udon* noodles, or for Chinese style noodles in broth.

□ *Wasabi* (Japanese horseradish) powder (sold in boxes or cans; illus. 3) can be used to make *wasabi* dip. Add some cold or tepid water to some *wasabi* powder to form a paste (use 3 tablespoons *wasabi* powder to 1-1/2 tablespoons water). Leave in a tightly sealed container for 10 minutes and it is ready for use.

炒烏龍麵

焼きうどん　　　4人份

■熟烏龍麵入開水川燙撈出。
■洋葱切絲，高麗菜葉梗片好（圖1）切絲，里肌肉切絲（圖2）。
■鍋熱入油3大匙，將洋葱絲、高麗菜絲及里肌肉絲略炒，續入1料及熟烏龍麵拌炒至汁收乾，淋上麻油及七味辣粉（圖3）即成。

| 熟烏龍麵4包 | ……………………1000公克 |
| 洋葱………………1個、里肌肉……150公克 |
| 高麗菜半個………………………300公克 |

	黑醋………2大匙、醬油………3大匙
1	味精……¼小匙、糖………1⅓大匙
	水………1½杯、胡椒………⅛小匙

麻油…………適量、七味辣粉………適量

FRIED UDON NOODLES

SERVES 4

■ Immerse the precooked *udon* noodles in boiling water briefly and remove.
■ Cut the onion into half-rings. Cut the cabbage heart into slices (illus. 1), then cut all of the cabbage into shreds. Cut the pork into shreds (illus. 2).
■ Heat a frying pan and add 3 tablespoons oil. Stir-fry the onion, cabbage, and pork briefly. Add 1 and the noodles. Stir-fry until the sauce is reduced. Sprinkle on a little sesame oil and seven-flavor seasoning (illus. 3), and serve.

4 packages (2 lb. 3 oz. or 1000 g) precooked *udon* noodles
1 onion
1/2 head cabbage (2/3 lb. or 300 g)
1/3 lb. (150 g) lean pork

1

2 T. Chinese dark vinegar
3 T. soy sauce, 1-1/3 T. sugar
1/4 t. MSG (optional)
1-1/2 c. water, 1/8 t. pepper
sesame oil, as desired
seven-flavor seasoning (*shichimi-tōgarashi*), as desired

溫泉蛋

温泉蛋　　　　4人份

雞蛋	4個
味醂	1½大匙
1 醬油	1大匙
煮出汁	⅔杯
柴魚片	4公克
貝芽菜	少許

■蛋放入冷水鍋中(圖1)，以小火煮約40分鐘，溫度保持65度至68度，溫度計不可碰到鍋底(圖2)，如溫度太高須加冷水或暫時熄火，待蛋黃呈半固體，蛋白呈滑嫩狀(圖3)，即成溫泉蛋。

■煮開1料即熄火，待柴魚片下沈後過濾，即為湯汁。

■將煮好的蛋去殼，每只置1個小碗中，上擺貝芽菜並注入湯汁即成。

□水溫65度至68度，約為開水4杯加冷水2½杯的溫度。

□煮好溫泉蛋置冰箱可保存2天，是一道精緻又富於變化的理想早餐。

HOT SPRING EGGS

SERVES 4

	4 eggs
	1-1/2 T. *mirin* (sweet rice wine)
	1 T. soy sauce
1	2/3 c. *dashi*
	1/8 oz. (4 g) bonito shavings (*hanagatsuo*)
	white radish sprouts (*kaiware*), as desired

■ Place the eggs in a saucepan of cold water (illus. 1) and cook about 40 minutes over low heat. The temperature should be maintained at between 149° to 154°F (65° to 68°C). Do not allow the thermometer to touch the bottom of the pot (illus. 2). Add cold water or temporarily turn off the heat if the temperature goes too high. Simmer until the yolk is partially solid, and the egg white is smooth and soft (illus. 3). These are "hot spring" eggs.

■ Bring 1 to a boil and turn off the flame immediately. Wait until the bonito shavings have settled, then strain. This is the soup stock.

■ Shell the cooked eggs, and place one egg in each bowl. Top with some white radish sprouts, add some soup stock, and serve.

□ 149° to 154°F (65° to 68°C) is equivalent to the temperature obtained by adding 4 cups boiling water to 2-1/2 cups cold water.

□ Hot spring eggs can be kept up to 2 days in the refrigerator. This dish is a delicate and unusual breakfast.

和風沙拉

和風サラダ　　　　　4人份

花枝 (不要剖開)	··········	400公克
	水	············ 6杯
	葱	············ 2枝
1	薑	············ 2片
	酒	·········· 1大匙
生菜	··········	1個
番茄	··········	1個
綠蘆筍	··········	12枝
洋葱	··········	1個
	沙拉油	············ 6大匙
	白醋	············ 2大匙
2	醬油	········· 1½大匙
	麻油	············ 1小匙
	白芝麻粉	········· 1大匙
熟蛋黃	··········	1個

■花枝去內臟及皮膜，放入煮開的１料內改小火燜煮３分鐘後熄火續燜３分鐘取出漂冷水 (使花枝肉脆硬適中)，切薄片呈環狀。

■生菜、番茄洗淨分別切片，綠蘆筍川燙切段，洋葱切圓片 (圖１) 浸冰水 (圖２) 約10分鐘，取出拭乾水份，２料拌勻成濃稠狀。

■將全部材料排整齊淋上２料，取過濾網置盤上方，將蛋黃磨碎 (圖３) 使其均勻落灑於蔬菜上即成。

JAPANESE SALAD

SERVES 4

14 oz. (400 g) cuttlefish (*ika*; do not split)

1
6 c. water
2 green onions
2 slices ginger root
1 T. rice wine
1 head lettuce
1 tomato
12 stalks fresh green asparagus
1 onion

2
6 T. salad oil
2 T. rice vinegar
1-1/2 T. soy sauce
1 t. sesame oil
1 T. white sesame seed powder
1 cooked egg yolk

■ Remove the entrails and outer membrane from the cuttlefish. Bring 1 to a boil and add the cuttlefish. Lower the heat and simmer, covered, for 3 minutes. Turn off the heat, then leave covered for another 3 minutes. Place in cold water (to make the cuttlefish firm). Cut into thin rings.

■ Wash the lettuce and tomato separately and cut into slices. Blanch the asparagus briefly in boiling water and cut into sections. Slice the onion into rounds (illus. 1) and soak in ice water (illus. 2) about 10 minutes. Remove from the ice water and pat dry with paper towels. Stir 2 together until of a thick consistency.

■ Arrange the salad ingredients neatly on a serving platter, then pour 2 over the top. Place the cooked egg yolk in a strainer and press down on the top with a rubber spatula to grate the yolk over the salad. Move the strainer while grating so that there is an even dusting of egg yolk over the top. Serve.

什錦煎

お好みやき　　　4人份

■ 1料全部置盆拌勻，即成濃稠適度的麵糊。將2料內的花枝切條（圖2），蝦仁去沙腸（圖3）。

■ 平底鍋燒熱，加油3大匙，倒入⅛的麵糊以小火煎成圓薄餅狀至半熟，撒上¼的2料，輕輕壓平，至底面略焦，翻面續煎1分鐘取出。另倒⅛的麵糊再煎一張圓薄餅至半熟，將前餅鏟至其上，續煎至兩面呈金黃色即可盛盤。

■ 食用時淋上調勻的3料，並灑上紅嫩薑絲、柴魚絲即可。

□ 炸天婦羅時撈起的碎渣即爲天婦羅屑。2料內加入天婦羅屑做出來的菜餡更香脆。如無可免用。

1	低筋麵粉	⅔杯
	煮出汁	¾杯、蛋 5個
2	高麗菜（切絲）	450公克
	天婦羅屑（圖1）	1杯
	花枝 150公克、蝦仁	150公克
	肉絲 75公克、葱花	½杯
3	芥茉醬 2小匙、番茄醬	6大匙
	沙拉醬 2大匙、黑醋	6～8大匙
	紅嫩薑絲 適量、柴魚絲	適量

SAVORY PANCAKES

SERVES 4

■ Mix 1 well to form a thick batter. Cut the cuttlefish in 2 into strips (illus. 2), and devein the shrimp (illus. 3).

■ Heat a flat-bottomed frying pan and add 3 tablespoons oil. Pour 1/8 of the batter into the pan and fry over low heat into a "pancake" until about half done. Sprinkle on 1/4 of 2, pressing the ingredients down lightly. When the bottom of the "pancake" is golden, turn it over to fry the other side for 1 minute. Remove to a plate with a spatula. Pour another 1/8 of the batter into the frying pan and again fry into a "pancake". Heat until about half done, then place the first "pancake" on top of the half-done second one. Continue to fry until golden brown. Transfer to a serving plate.

■ Mix 3 until blended. Top the pancake with 3, then some pickled red ginger root shreds and bonito shreds. Serve.

□ "Tempura crumbs" are the crumbs of fried batter which are skimmed from the oil when frying *tempura*. Adding *tempura* crumbs to 2 gives this dish extra flavor and crunch. They may be omitted if unavailable.

1	2/3 c. low-gluten flour
	3/4 c. *dashi*
	5 eggs
2	1 lb. (450 g) cabbage, shredded
	1 c. *tempura* crumbs (illus. 1)
	1/3 lb. (150 g) cuttlefish (*ika*)
	1/3 lb. (150 g) shrimp (shelled)
	2-1/2 oz. (75 g) pork shreds
	1/2 c. chopped green onion
3	2 t. mustard, 6 T. ketchup
	2 T. mayonaise
	6-8 T. Chinese dark vinegar
	pickled red ginger root (*beni-shōga*) shreds, as desired
	fine bonito shreds (*hanagatsuo*), as desired

牛肉煎蛋

スコツチオムレツ　　4人份

牛絞肉	………………………	200公克
洋葱	………………………	½個
青花菜	………………………	150公克
紅蘿蔔	………………………	½條
1	荳蔲粉（圖1） ………………	¼小匙
	胡椒粉、塩 ………………	各⅛小匙
	奶油…… 8大匙、麵粉……	2小匙
	甜酒（圖2） ………………	2大匙
蛋	………………………	8個

■洋葱切碎（圖3），青花菜修飾成小朶花，紅蘿蔔切粗條，分別放入開水中煮約3分鐘，取出漂涼，瀝乾水份。

■平底鍋燒熱，加奶油2大匙，將洋葱炒軟，續入牛絞肉略拌，調上1料拌勻，即爲餡。

■蛋兩個加塩及胡椒粉各⅒小匙打勻。

■平底鍋燒熱，加奶油1½大匙，倒入蛋汁略拌，輕輕壓平待凝成直徑18公分之半固體，再以中火烘成圓餅狀，入¼的餡，視蛋皮底部略焦即對摺熄火，鏟出盛盤，旁置青花菜及紅蘿蔔即成。餘6個蛋以同樣方法煎成。

□如無荳蔲粉可免用。

JAPANESE BEEF OMELETTE

SERVES 4

	7 oz. (200 g) ground beef
	1/2 onion
	1/3 lb. (150 g) broccoli
	1/2 carrot
1	1/4 t. nutmeg (illus. 1)
	1/8 t. pepper
	1/8 t. salt
	8 T. butter
	2 t. flour
	2 T. sweet wine (illus. 2)
	8 eggs

■ Chop the onion (illus. 3). Cut the broccoli into flowerets, and the carrot into thick strips. Immerse each separately in boiling water for about 3 minutes. Place in cold water to stop the cooking process, then drain.

■ Heat a flat-bottomed frying pan, then add 2 tablespoons butter. Sauté the onion in the butter until soft, add the ground beef, and mix well. Mix 1 into the beef mixture until well combined. This is the filling.

■ Add 1/10 teaspoon each salt and pepper to 2 of the eggs. Beat lightly to mix in.

■ Heat the frying pan and add 1-1/2 tablespoons butter. Pour in the egg and stir gently. Lightly press down on the egg when it is about half set to form a pancake 7" (18 cm) in diameter. Bake over medium heat until fully set. Add 1/4 of the filling and fold in half when the bottom of the egg "pancake" begins to brown. Turn off the heat and transfer to a serving plate. Place some broccoli and carrot on the side. Repeat the same procedure for the 6 remaining eggs. Serve.

□ The nutmeg is optional, and may be omitted if unavailable.

鐵板燒

牛肉	400公克		醬油	¾杯
蝦8條	300公克		煮出汁	¾杯
花枝1條	300公克	2	味酥	4大匙
青椒	4個		糖	2大匙
香菇(大)	7朵		味精	少許
洋葱	1個		白芝麻粉	1杯
茄子	1條		白味噌	少許
1 ┌ 白蘿蔔	½條	3	醬油	¾杯
└ 紅辣椒	1條		味酥	2小匙
檸檬汁	適量		葱末	2大匙

■將牛肉切0.5公分薄片,蝦洗淨(或去背殼留頭尾殼),花枝切花刀,青椒去籽切塊,香菇泡軟切塊,洋葱切圓片,茄子切斜片,1料磨成泥(參考第42頁鮮魚蒸豆腐)備用。
■備鐵板鍋,塗上少許油(或牛油),取適量材料一面煎一面食用,並任選2料或3料作爲沾汁(汁內酌加1料及檸檬汁)。

TEPPANYAKI

14 oz. (400 g) beef
8 shrimp (2/3 lb. or 300 g)
1 cuttlefish (2/3 lb. or 300 g) — 2
4 green peppers
7 large dried Chinese black mushrooms (*shiitake*)
1 onion
1 eggplant (preferably long thin Oriental) — 3
1 ┌ 1/2 Chinese white radish (*daikon*)
└ 1 small red chili pepper

3/4 c. each: soy sauce, *dashi*
4 T. *mirin* (sweet rice wine)
2 T. sugar
pinch of MSG (optional)

1 c. white sesame seed powder
bit of white *miso*
3/4 c. soy sauce
2 t. *mirin*
2 T. minced green onion

lemon juice, as desired

■ Cut the beef into 3/8″ (1 cm) thick slices. Wash the shrimp (the shells may be removed from the body portion, head and tail left intact). Score the cuttlefish with a crosscut. Seed the green pepper and cut into pieces. Soak the dried mushroom until soft and cut into pieces. Cut the onion into rounds, and the eggplant into diagonal slices. Grind 1 into a puree (see p. 42, Fresh Fish Steamed with Tofu). Set aside.
■ Lightly oil (or butter) an iron *teppanyaki* griddle. Fry the ingredients (in a quantity appropriate for the size of the griddle), and eat as the food becomes ready. Dip in 2 or 3. A little 1 and lemon juice may be added to the dipping sauce.

MORE FROM WEI-CHUAN PUBLISHING

COOKBOOKS :

ALL COOKBOOKS ARE BILINGUAL (ENGLISH/CHINESE) UNLESS FOOTNOTED OTHERWISE

Apetizers, Chinese Style
Chinese Appetizers & Garnishes
Chinese Cooking, Favorite Home Dishes
Chinese Cooking For Beginners (Rev.) [1]
Chinese Cooking Made Easy
Chinese Cuisine
Chinese Cuisine-Cantonese Style
Chinese Cuisine-Shanghai Style
Chinese Cuisine-Szechwan Style
Chinese Cuisine-Taiwanese Style
Chinese Dim Sum
Chinese Herb Cooking for Health
Chinese Home Cooking for Health
Chinese One Dish Meals (Rev.) [3]
Chinese Snacks (Rev.)
Favorite Chinese Dishes
Fish [3]

Great Garnishes
Healthful Cooking
Indian Cuisine
International Baking Delights
Japanese Cuisine
Low Cholesterol Chinese Cuisine
Mexican Cooking Made Easy [4]
Noodles, Chinese Home-Cooking
Noodles, Classical Chinese Cooking [3]
One Dish Meals; From Popular Cuisines [3]
Rice, Chinese Home-Cooking
Rice, Traditional Chinese Cooking
Shellfish [3]
Simply Vegetarian
Thai Cooking Made Easy
Vegetarian Cooking

SMALL COOKBOOK SERIES

Beef [2]
Chicken [2]
Soup! Soup! Soup!
Tofu! Tofu! Tofu!
Vegetables [2]
Very! Very! Vegetarian!

VIDEOS

Chinese Garnishes I [5]
Chinese Garnishes II [5]
Chinese Stir-Frying: Beef [5]
Chinese Stir-Frying: Chicken [5]
Chinese Stir-Frying: Vegetables [5]

OTHERS

Carving Tools

---

1 Also available in English/Spanish, French/Chinese, and German/Chinese
2 English and Chinese are in separate editions
3 Trilingual English/Chinese/Spanish edition

4 Also available in English/Spanish
5 English Only

Wei-Chuan Cookbooks can be purchased in the U.S.A., Canada and twenty other countries worldwide
1455 Monterey Pass Road, #110, Monterey Park, CA 91754, U.S.A. • Tel: (323) 261-3880 • Fax: (323) 261-3299

味全叢書

食譜系列

(如無數字標註，即為中英對照版)

美味小菜
拼盤與盤飾
實用家庭菜
實用中國菜(修訂版)[1]
速簡中國菜
中國菜
廣東菜
上海菜
四川菜

台灣菜
飲茶食譜
養生藥膳
養生家常菜
簡餐專輯(修訂版)[3]
點心專輯
家常100
魚[3]
盤飾精選

健康食譜
印度菜
實用烘焙
日本料理
均衡飲食
墨西哥菜[4]
麵，家常篇
麵，精華篇
簡餐(五國風味)[3]

米食，家常篇
米食，傳統篇
蝦、貝、蟹[3]
健康素
泰國菜
素食

味全小食譜

牛肉[2]
雞肉[2]
蔬菜[2]

湯
豆腐
家常素食

錄影帶

盤飾 I [5]
盤飾 II [5]

炒菜入門，牛肉[5]
炒菜入門，雞肉[5]
炒菜入門，蔬菜[5]

其他

雕花刀

---

1 中英、英西、中法、中德版　　2 中文版及英文版　　3 中、英、西對照版　　4 英西版　　5 英文版

味全食譜在台、美加及全球二十餘國皆有發行 • 味全出版社有限公司 • 台北市仁愛路4段28號2樓
Tel:(02)2702-1148 • Fax:(02)2704-2729

OTROS LIBROS DE WEI-CHUAN

EDICIONES EN ESPAÑOL

Cocina China Para Principiantes, Edición Revisada [1]
Cocina Popular de Un Solo Platillo [2]
Comida China de Un Solo Platillo, Edición Revisada [2]
Comida Mexicana, Fácil de Preparar [3]
Mariscos, Estilo Chino Fácil de Preparar [2]
Pescado, Estilo Chino Fácil de Preparar [2]

---

1 Disponible en Inglés/Español, Inglés/Chino, Francés/Chino, y Alemán/Chino
2 Edición trilingüe Inglés/Chino/Español
3 Disponible en ediciones bilingües Inglés/Español e Inglés/Chino

Los Libros de Cocina Wei-Chuan se pueden comprar en E.E.U.U., Canadá y otros 20 países a través del mundo.
1455 Monterey Pass Road, #110, Monterey Park, CA 91754, U.S.A. • Tel: (323) 261-3880 • Fax: (323) 261-3299